SKILLS WITH PEOPLE
A GUIDE FOR MANAGERS

SKILLS WITH PEOPLE

A GUIDE FOR MANAGERS

Elizabeth Sidney
Margaret Brown and
Michael Argyle

HUTCHINSON OF LONDON

HUTCHINSON & CO (*Publishers*) LTD
3 Fitzroy Square, London W1

London Melbourne Sydney Auckland
Wellington Johannesburg Cape Town
and agencies throughout the world

First published 1973

© Elizabeth Sidney, Margaret Brown and Michael Argyle 1973

*This book has been set in Times type, printed in Great Britain
on antique wove paper by Anchor Press, and
bound by Wm. Brendon, both of Tiptree, Essex*

ISBN 0 09 116480 X (cased)
     0 09 116481 8 (paper)

CONTENTS

Contents

PREFACE

Management and administration involve a number of special-ised professional skills. Skills with people are among the most important of these—managers spend about two-thirds of their working time with other people. These social skills are not things that can be picked up in everyday life; they require special analysis, research into the best techniques, and training in how to perform them.

There has been a great deal of research into social skills, and social behaviour at work, during recent years. This research tells us a lot about the best ways to handle different situations and relationships at work. Those of us who do this research always hope that use will be made of it; very often it remains buried in the journals.

Elizabeth Sidney, Margaret Brown and myself thought of this book as a kind of 'Spock' for managers—describing the most effective social skills for different kinds of interview, taking the chair at meetings, leading groups, etc. In addition we have tried to give some understanding of the processes involved, both in individual social performance and inside working groups. We have drawn on a very extensive body of carefully conducted research, which has produced clear-cut and widely confirmed findings in many areas. Research shows how much the effectiveness of interviewers, leaders, etc., varies between different performers, and that it depends on the specific social skills used. These findings do not always agree with current practices in industry, or with the doctrines which are now fashionable among consultants, and embodied in management theories.

Of course it takes more than reading actually to acquire these skills—though reading can give deeper understanding of what is happening in social situations. We have all been

Preface

involved in the development of methods of training in social skills for some years, and the first two authors are very experienced in teaching management skills. We discuss follow-up studies which compare the before-and-after effectiveness of those who have experienced different kinds of training. We now know that many people fail to learn the right social skills by experience on the job, and that social skills can be learnt, and fairly rapidly, by specially designed training experiences. Training courses usually need special materials, and we have produced an example of these in a set of films, tapes, etc. (*Selection Interviewing Training Programme*, Mantra, 1969).

We have not produced a complete bibliography to the numerous studies referred to in the text. Instead we thought that it would be more useful to give carefully selected references to further reading at the end of each chapter. We also give check lists at the end of those chapters where the contents can usefully be summarised in action.

We are greatly indebted to many colleagues and friends, who have been involved in the research reported here, or collaborated in training courses. I should also thank the SSRC and the Oxford Regional Hospital Board for financial support for my own research.

Michael Argyle
Department of Experimental Psychology, Oxford
May, 1973

1

INTRODUCTION

Why managers need social skills

Most work is done in groups and organisations, and most people at work have to spend a good deal of time communicating in some way with other people in order to achieve the necessary coordination of effort. This is true of manual workers, research workers and everyone else in a working organisation. However, it is particularly true of managers, who spend something like 65 per cent of their time with others in a variety of different situations and relationships. Communicating is not the whole of a manager's job and social skills are not the only skills he needs, but this is a very important part of his work.

We define social skills as the ways in which a person behaves towards others in different social situations. Examples would be how a manager conducts an interview or a committee meeting or how he deals with an individual or group over a period of time. Just as some ways of performing a manual skill produce better results, so do certain ways of conducting social situations and managing social relationships.

The effect may be immediate—for example, the manager may be able to handle individuals or groups in such a way that they immediately work more efficiently, or the effect may be long-term—for example, he may be able to select the right candidate for a post even though the benefits of this appointment will not be fully realised for some years.

A lot is known about the skills of manual workers. Manual jobs are studied, the best way of doing each job is found out, and carefully designed training courses are given to teach the necessary skills. By contrast, managers usually receive very little training or instruction in the social skills which they must exercise; they are expected to pick them up on the job. It is true that everyday social skills are normally learnt by experience. However, it is now known that this is a very unreliable kind of training, whereby some people fail to learn much at all, and others even learn the wrong ways of handling people. It is our view that managerial skills are specific and complex professional skills, which are not picked up in everyday life and for which special training is needed. It is rather paradoxical that so much effort has been devoted to training manual workers rather than to training managers in their respective skills, in view of the fact that managers have a far greater influence on the productivity of an enterprise. The reason is that until quite recently very little was known about the nature of social skills, or the skills which are most effective in work situations. Now that this knowledge has become available it is possible to devise training in the styles of behaviour which are known to be effective.

The idea that social skills are important is not new. Elton Mayo maintained that social skills were the key to industrial problems; he was referring mainly to supervisory skills. The American social scientists who produced what is commonly known as the Human Relations Movement also emphasised supervisory skills and the importance of cooperative working groups. In recent years there has been an upsurge of interest in various forms of social-skills training—T-groups and other kinds of group experience. Our approach is somewhat different in that we shall deal with a series of specific managerial social skills rather than with social competence in general. We shall also, after considering these specific skills, look at the social environment in which the manager works, which can affect his ability to use these skills.

The social skills needed by managers

Managers have to deal with a number of specific situations involving short-term relationships—various kinds of interviewing, speaking and writing, and committee work. They also have to deal with various long-term relationships—as leader, as team member and in dealing with individuals.

Managers have to deal with individuals, with small groups, and with larger groups. They have to deal with those above and below them in the organisation, with trade union representatives and with customers and clients from outside the firm. They may have to persuade, instruct, negotiate, buy and sell, or give personal help. For each of these different relationships and tasks different managerial skills are needed. There has been a great deal of research into some of these skills during recent years, as well as more basic research into the fundamental processes of social behaviour. For example, there has been extensive research into the skills of handling working groups, and we now know the specific social skills which produce the best results. These skills are by no means obvious to common-sense, and involve a rather subtle combination of ways of interacting with others. The research has also shown the magnitude of the effects produced, and the variation in techniques needed under different social conditions (Chapter 7). There have been important developments in the methods of training people in these skills and careful before- and after-studies have been made of all the different methods of training—some of which have been found to be quite useless. This is discussed in Chapter 9.

The influence of social skills on organisational effectiveness

What do we mean by saying that some kinds of behaviour are more effective than others? The simplest answer is that behaviour is effective if it achieves its intended purpose, e.g. an interviewer assesses the candidate accurately so that the latter subsequently performs as expected when appointed to the job. In research on styles of supervision it has been shown that supervision affects productivity (rate of useful work), absenteeism, labour turnover and measures of job satisfaction.

13

In this book we shall describe behaviour as 'effective' in relation to what the behaviour is intended to achieve and the results it has been shown to produce. Neither the purpose nor the results will always seem desirable to all managers. For example, a manager might argue that behaviour which encourages everyone to produce new ideas, when there is no possibility of implementing them, would be positively undesirable. Some kinds of supervisory behaviour increase job satisfaction and others increase productivity: unfortunately, the two do not always go hand-in-hand. Most social scientists think that job satisfaction is of great importance simply on humanitarian grounds. A manager, however, might see supervisory behaviour which increased output as more desirable than different behaviour which increased worker satisfaction. In certain conditions of shortage of skilled labour, it may be of paramount importance to keep labour turnover to a minimum, even at the expense of other goals. Effective supervisory behaviour in these circumstances would be any behaviour which deterred skilled staff from leaving.

Our concern here is not to uphold particular objectives but to present the social skills which will lead to all kinds of organisational effectiveness. When we recommend certain social techniques, this is not to suggest that managers 'ought' to behave in these ways for some moral reason. The basis of these recommendations will be simply that certain social skills have as a matter of fact been found to lead to better results, according to their objective—whether greater productivity, lower absenteeism, lower accident rates, etc. There is extensive evidence, which we quote in this book, to show that different social skills are effective in different ways. In some cases the effect is very marked. For example, untrained and unskilled interviewers do only marginally better than chance. while trained ones do very much better. In various ways, the use of different social skills will have a direct effect on productivity—for example, in selecting the right people, in

14

communicating with them more clearly, in handling individuals and groups more successfully and in generating more co-operation. Some social behaviour makes life more enjoyable for subordinates and colleagues than others, and so contributes to job satisfaction. Social skills are not a luxury: they have a great effect on all aspects of organisational effectiveness.

Do social skills entail manipulation?

A *New Yorker* cartoon showed a group of managers watching one of their colleagues being shown out of the office by their boss, who was smiling warmly and had his arm round his visitor's shoulders: they commented 'I see Jones didn't get that rise'. This makes a cynical comment on the use of kindly and democratic styles of supervision and management (described in Chapter 7) suggesting that their real purpose is to manipulate people, persuading them to responses and courses of action which may not be what they actually wish to do. Behind the joke is a real fear sometimes openly expressed as a reason for rejecting training in social skills. In a book dedicated to the concept that social skills can, and indeed should, be consciously learned, this fear must be discussed at the outset.

Of course when people learn a social skill they will have an objective, and because the skill is to do with their relationship to others, the objective is likely to be to make others respond in some required way. This is true of skills learned from experience. A child learns to ingratiate himself or to bully, to conform or rebel according to the response this provokes from his parents. Boys learn behaviours intended to attract girls and vice versa. One defence of training in social skills is that it simply raises to the conscious level a process which is going on, more or less clumsily or effectively, all the time.

Another possible defence is that many of the objectives of the performer do meet the needs of those with whom he interacts. For example, a kindly and democratic style of supervision certainly produces more cooperation and productivity. But it also makes subordinates happier. In this type of supervision there is a genuine concern for the welfare of subordinates, and they are invited to participate in decisions, partly because this will lead to better decisions being made, and also because they appreciate being consulted, and because they will implement the decisions made more willingly. Similarly, an industrial salesman is concerned to discover the detailed needs of his client and tries to meet these needs from his company's resources. A speaker or teacher wants to produce a clear, accurate and interesting account of what he has to present, and this is precisely what his listeners would like him to do. In many management situations it is perfectly possible to maximise productivity and satisfaction at the same time. Although rather different methods of handling are needed to promote these two aims, the managerial techniques involved are entirely compatible.

These are sound defences, but they do not resolve all the difficulties. The fact is that social skills, like any other skills, can be used for 'good' or 'evil' purposes. A surgeon could use his skill to mutilate rather than cure, and would be able to do so with greater subtlety and effectiveness than someone without surgical training. Brainwashing is a crude example of how relationships are manipulated to serve 'undesirable' ends. In our view, the best defence against misuse of social skills lies in the awareness (but not the automatic cynicism) expressed in the *New Yorker* cartoon.

How far should social skills vary with technology and organisation?

Many of the findings to be reported later about the most effective social skills have an impressive degree of generality. Similar findings have been obtained in a wide variety of industrial settings, and in different cultures. Nevertheless, the precise skills which produce the best results have been found to vary somewhat with the technology and organisation. For example, a superior's ability to exercise supervisory skill is profoundly affected by the layout of the shop he supervises, the number of workers, the type of work they do, etc. In fact, it must be recognised that all interpersonal skills must be exercised within the framework of the total working situation. A meeting is profoundly affected by the adequacy of its terms of reference, whether members come as delegates or representatives, and so on.

Recent research and thinking have emphasised the technological and organisational features of the work setting. We shall consider how far the skills used need to vary with different kinds of technology and organisation. We shall also consider the ways in which the organisation may be modified to enhance effectiveness; part of managerial skill consists of designing the best organisational structures. This is discussed in Chapter 8. Recent experimental research into social behaviour has led to the discovery of a number of fundamental processes, which operate in all social situations, and which help one to understand and deal with them. These are discussed in Chapter 2.

We have to deal with social skills in a particular cultural setting. The research findings which we have used were obtained in Britain, Europe or the USA during the period 1950–72, and the generality of the skills recommended is restricted to this cultural area. They might work in Africa or Japan, but this cannot be assumed without further research. Some social skills have already been shown to have some cross-cultural validity (e.g. styles of supervision), and some non-verbal signals are similar in all cultures (e.g. facial expression of emotions). However, there are important differences between cultures and these are bound to affect social skills in some ways.

We hope that this book will help those who study it to deal with people and social situations at work more easily and with greater effect. We also hope that it will help them to enjoy more their dealings with others, in the work situation and outside it.

Further reading

An excellent account of American research in the "Human Relations tradition is given in:

> R. Likert, *New Patterns of Management* (McGraw-Hill, New York, 1961)

An account of research on social skills and other aspects of social behaviour at work, set in a broad biological and historical setting, is given in:

> Michael Argyle, *The Social Psychology of Work* (Allen Lane, The Penguin Press, 1972)

2
THE BASIC PRINCIPLES OF SOCIAL BEHAVIOUR

In this chapter we shall start by describing the basic signals of which all basic behaviour consists. This is intended to 'sensitise' the reader to some of the subtleties of social behaviour. We shall then describe some of the basic principles which govern all kinds of social behaviour, including an account of social skills, social behaviour at work, and social competence.

The elements of social behaviour

Human social behaviour consists partly of talk, partly of non-verbal communication, which plays several important roles in our social behaviour. Here are the main non-verbal elements, together with brief notes on what they communicate:

Bodily contact. In Britain in the work situation this is largely confined to greetings and farewells, though there is much more inside the family. Bodily contact is used more in a number of other cultures, and more of it may be expected by overseas clients, for example from Arab or African countries.

Proximity. There are cultural rules about how close to each other people should sit or stand. The English are more distant than Latin Americans, Arabs or Southern Italians, but less distant than the Scots or Swedes for example. People get closer to those they like, and maladjusted people tend to be more distant.

Orientation. We indicate our attitudes to others by our physical orientation to them. Side-by-side indicates cooperation, head-on shows opposition, while 90 degrees is chosen for many kinds of discussion. We also signal the beginning and end of an encounter—turning towards someone indicates a desire to speak to him.

Head-nods. Nodding indicates agreement and encourages another person in what he is saying or doing; it is also one of the signals controlling synchronising—it gives the other person permission to continue speaking.

Facial expression. This is a form of non-verbal expression which is carefully controlled, so that it may be difficult to penetrate to true feelings and attitudes. However, facial expression often communicates a continuous commentary on what others are saying, showing surprise, disbelief, anger, agreement, disappointment, etc. A manager can learn much about the true feelings of others if he learns to study and interpret the facial expressions of colleagues, customers, subordinates and superiors.

Gesture. Gestures, especially of the hands, are closely coordinated with speech, and affect the meaning of utterances. General emotional arousal produces diffuse bodily movements, specific emotional states produce gestures like clenching the fists in anger. Some of these specific gestures are partly innate. Few of us have difficulty in interpreting the meaning of a general rustling of papers at a committee meeting, where someone is holding forth at inordinate length.

Posture. There are characteristic postures for friendly, hostile, inferior and superior attitudes, and posture is one of the main cues showing attitudes towards another person. For example, a person may signal or try to establish dominance by standing erect with unsmiling face, voice loud and assertive.

Direction of gaze. Looking plays several important roles in social behaviour. People look primarily to obtain information and feedback from others, and look about twice as much while listening as while talking. The act of looking also indicates the amount and kind of interest the looker has at the other; long periods of looking indicates a desire for intimacy, and people look more when further apart, to compensate for the separation. The facial expression indicates whether the interest is primarily affiliative, sexual, hostile, etc. Shifts of gaze are also used to regulate the synchronising of speech—for example a speaker gives a prolonged look just before the ending of an utterance.

Appearance. Physical grooming and choice of clothes are largely under voluntary control. They are used to present impressions about the status, occupation and personality of the wearer and to show how he would like to be treated. Long hair, beards and psychedelic ties worn by many younger men in industry today signal their affiliation to the culture of the younger generation. Other young men wear striped trousers and bowler hats. Members of each group are making statements about their values and their group membership.

Non-verbal aspects of speech. Variations of pitch, stress and timing are an integral part of speech and affect the meaning of utterances. Variations in voice quality communicate the emotional state of the speaker, his attitude to the listener (e.g., inferior, hostile), his personality, or his cultural background. For example, when a speaker puts great emphasis on some word in a sentence, he is usually conveying that he feels strongly about something. It is often easier to learn about another person's emotional state from his tone of voice than from his facial expression, which tends to be better controlled.

The contents of speech. The three main kinds of utterances are questions, orders and information. We can distinguish between formal conversation, which is primarily concerned with information exchange and problem-solving, and informal conversation, which is more concerned with establishing, maintaining, and enjoying interpersonal relationships. Remarks

21

may be worded so that latent messages are conveyed, for example about the importance of the speaker, or his relationship to his hearers. There are a number of special kinds of talk, such as jokes, and talk about talk as in T-groups. Particular management skills require specialised kinds of talk, such as tactfully enquiring about the candidate's failures in a selection interview, asking the other to give his side of the story in a personnel interview, and motivating subordinates by supervisors. An important part of social skill consists in the formulation of the most effective utterances, closely linked with and supported by non-verbal signals.

The links between verbal and non-verbal signals

Animals conduct their entire social life by means of non-verbal signals, which are similar to those used by man. In man, non-verbal signals act in three main ways—to support and sustain verbal communication, to manage the immediate social situation, and to replace verbal communication.

NON-VERBAL SUPPORT OF VERBAL COMMUNICATION

An authority on linguistics, Abercrombie, said, 'We speak with our vocal organs but we converse with our whole body.' Non-verbal signals play several crucial roles in verbal communication.

Vocal and gestural signals which affect the meaning of utterances. A person would not be accepted as speaking the language properly unless he delivered his utterance in the appropriate pitch, stress and temporal pattern for that language. The meaning of a sentence depends on these non-verbal aspects of speech, which indicate phrase-boundaries and grammatical structure, give emphasis to particular words, indicate whether the utterance is a serious statement, a question, intended to be funny, sarcastic, etc. Much the same is true of the gestural and facial accompaniments of speech, which also display the grammatical structure, show emphasis, and comment on the utterance. In addition they can modify meaning, as when the speaker points to persons or objects, or illustrates what is being spoken of. Visual signals can also warn the listener of what is to come. Speech is accompanied by continuous movements of hands and body; these movements have a hierarchical structure coordinated to the structure of speech: while a large verbal unit such as a paragraph is accompanied by a steady posture, smaller units like sentences and words are accompanied by finer movements of the head and fingers.

Controlling the synchronising of speech. When two or more people are talking they must take it in turns to speak, and they usually manage to achieve a fairly smooth 'synchronising' sequence, without interruptions or silences. This is done by means of a simple non-verbal code consisting of head-nods, shifts of gaze, grunts and hand-movements. For example at a grammatical pause a speaker will look up to see if the others are willing for him to carry on speaking; if they are they will nod and grunt.

Feedback. A speaker needs intermittent information on how others are responding, so that he can modify his remarks if necessary. This is mainly obtained from study of the other's eyebrows and mouth which indicate surprise, disbelief, etc. On the telephone these signals are transferred to the auditory channel.

Signalling attentiveness. Interactors must provide continuous evidence that they are attending to the others. This is done by adopting an appropriate proximity, orientation and posture, frequent gaze at the other, head-nods, and facial expressions and bodily movements which are responsive to the other's speech and bodily movements.

Skills with people

Like animals we conduct our social relationships primarily by non-verbal signals.

Signalling interpersonal attitudes. Attitudes such as friendly–hostile and inferior–superior are conveyed by posture, facial expression and tone of voice. Experiments by Argyle and co-workers found that if previously equated verbal and non-verbal cues for such attitudes are combined, the non-verbal cues have about five times the effect of the verbal; where they are in conflict the verbal cues are ignored. To indicate that you like someone it is more effective to smile, look, sit side-by-side, adopt the appropriate tone of voice, and perhaps touch him, than to try to put it into words.

Emotional states. These are communicated by tone of voice, facial expression, posture, gestures and pattern of gaze. Interactors may try to conceal their emotions, but some of these cues are very difficult to control since they reflect the physiological state of the body. Again an interactor has no need to announce that he is happy, anxious or depressed; it is enough that his tone of voice and facial expression show his emotional condition.

Self-presentation. This can be done by words, but is not socially acceptable in many cultures. The normal signals are appearance, non-verbal aspects of speech (e.g., accent and manner of talking), and general style of verbal and non-verbal performance.

NON-VERBAL REPLACEMENT OF VERBAL
COMMUNICATION

When verbal communication is impossible for some reason, non-verbal gesture languages are developed to replace it. This happens in broadcasting, between underwater swimmers and on racecourses. Gesture languages develop in noisy factories, as does skill at lip-reading. Matters of a confidential nature can then be 'overheard' at the other end of the room if the speaker forgets to turn his back or to hold his hand in front of his mouth.

Social performance as a motor skill

We now come to a topic of central importance to this book. We have listed the main elements of social behaviour, and shown how verbal and non-verbal signals are coordinated. We shall now look at the performance of a single interactor, and show that he emits a sequence of verbal and non-verbal signals intended to control the behaviour of others, and bring about some desired state of affairs. The following discussion will be concerned with encounters between two persons, who may be manager and subordinate, salesman and client, interviewer and candidate, and so on; we shall refer to them, for brevity, as A and B.

In the first place there are certain regular sequences, whereby an act by A is usually followed by some act by B—so that A can use this sequence to control B. Here are some examples of such sequences: (1) A asks a question—B answers it. If A asks a closed question, B will give a short reply; if A asks an open-ended question, B will give a long reply. (2) A reinforces B—B repeats the act reinforced. For example, if A nods, smiles, looks, leans forward, or makes encouraging noises when B has said or done something, B will do this more often; negative responses by A will result in B doing it less often. This process occurs very rapidly, and often without the awareness of either. Each person is constantly influencing the other, and being influenced by him, since each reacts spontaneously in a positive or negative manner to the behaviour of the other. (3) Any act of A's is likely to be repeated by B. For example, if A nods his head, interrupts, smiles, laughs, yawns, etc., B is likely to do the same. Sometimes this is due to imitation, sometimes to reciprocity—the deliberate exchange

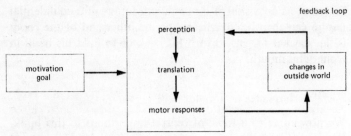

Fig. 2.1.

of gifts. (4) If A uses non-verbal signals corresponding to interpersonal attitudes, B is likely to accept the relationship offered. For example, if A adopts a 'superior' manner—unsmiling, erect posture, loud and dominant voice—B is likely to adopt an 'inferior' role. The same is true of friendly or hostile interpersonal attitudes.

A sequence of social interaction cannot be understood simply in terms of individuals making and responding to signals from one another. Each has a plan, and emits an organised sequence of signals. Each interactor is motivated to attain certain goals, such as some desired response on the part of the other, and continuously modifies his behaviour in the light of feedback to reach them. In these and other ways social behaviour resembles the performance of a manual skill, like driving a car. The elements of the motor-skill model are shown in Fig. 2.1. The motivation of a social performer may be to persuade the other to perform a task (as in supervision), to produce information (interview), to buy something (selling), to learn something (teaching), and so on. These are the performer's professional goals; he will also have social needs such as wanting to be liked or admired.

PERCEPTION

A skilled performer learns which cues to attend to, and becomes highly sensitive to them. He is primarily concerned

26

with feedback cues, i.e., cues giving information about how the other person is responding. The car driver looks at the road, other traffic and his instruments; a social-skill performer looks at the face and hands of the other, and listens to his voice. He looks the other intermittently in the area of the eyes, to study the other's direction of gaze and his facial expression; he always looks at the ends of his utterances, since this is when feedback is most needed—on how the other has reacted to an utterance.

MOTOR RESPONSES

The social performance consists of an integrated sequence of verbal and non-verbal responses. A particular performance, such as giving an interview or taking the chair at a meeting, has a series of sub-goals or stages; for example, an interviewer usually starts by establishing rapport and explaining the procedure. Each stage has components of its own, and the skill consists of a series of units, each complete in itself, each with its own sub-goals and feedback loop. Each unit consists of a hierarchical structure of smaller units. While the larger units are carefully planned, the smaller units are habitual and unthinking—we do not have to think about how to utter each word.

FEEDBACK AND CORRECTIVE ACTION

The performer keeps continual watch on how the other is responding, and takes corrective action, to the best of his ability, in order to produce the reactions he is seeking in the other. When the other's reaction has been perceived, it is necessary to know what to do about it. A boat goes off course to the left, so the helmsman pulls the right-hand rope; a candidate being interviewed talks too little, so what does the interviewer do? This kind of information is acquired during the learning of a skill and is stored in the brain. It may take the form of verbalised principles of behaviour, e.g., 'If the other person talks too little, ask open-ended questions and reinforce his utterances by head-nods and sounds of approval'. Or it may be stored in a less cognitive form and consist of habitual response patterns. Or it may start in a verbalised form and later become automatic. A skilled interviewer can get a candidate talking the right amount and on the desired topics from the outset of the interview. Similarly a chairman can keep a tight control over a meeting by such devices as frequent summaries, by asking for individual contributions round the table, by a rigid procedural plan, by imposing time limits and so on. A person with very high social skill can exercise precise control over the other's amount of talking, his emotional state, the degree of intimacy, relative dominance he feels, and so on.

TAKING THE ROLE OF THE OTHER

However there is more to social performance than the skilled manipulation of another's responses. Interactors 'take the role of the other', i.e., imagine the other's point of view, in different degrees, and with varying accuracy.

It may be that taking the role of the other is necessary for effective social performance. Several measures of the *ability* to take the role of the other have been devised; in one experiment it was found that subjects who did well at such a test were also more effective in a two-person communication task. Studies of sympathy and helping behaviour have found that a person is more likely to help another in distress if he has experienced that kind of distress himself.

A manager's ability to think himself into the role of another is a key requirement for the success of his job. This basic skill underlines all the other particular skills which we discuss later in this book. It is particularly important when communicating, persuading or negotiating. Communications, to be effective, need to be couched in the language and to be addressed to the attitudes and needs of the recipient. Equally, before we can persuade another to accept an idea or a course of action, we have to understand the nature of his individual needs, situation and problems and keep these in mind. At the negotiating table the manager's success will partly depend on his ability to understand the true meaning of the words being used by his shop stewards or the local district official, and to remember the pressures that they are under.

EQUILIBRIUM PROCESSES

Two or more individuals must behave in a highly coordinated way for there to be any interaction at all. There must be coordination over (1) the content of interaction, i.e., the nature of the activity or the topic of conversation, (2) the role-relations and definition of the situation, e.g., whether it is to be a casual chat, a job interview, or vocational guidance, (3) how intimate the encounter is, (4) the dominance relations, (5) the emotional tone, (6) the proper sequence of acts, e.g., questions should lead to answers, gestures should be responded to etc., (7) the timing and amounts of speech. To work out a pattern of interaction between two or more people requires some rapid group problem-solving; this problem-solving is carried out mainly by the use of minor non-verbal cues.

Small attempts may be made at intimacy or dominance, with careful study of how another reacts, so that these can be withdrawn if his reaction is too negative. A sufficient supply of rewards must be delivered to the other in order to keep him in the situation. Encounters often begin with a period of informal chat, whose purpose is probably to enable some degree of synchronising to be established.

Many of these equilibrium processes can be observed in the early stages of a new committee. Opening gambits, watchful waiting, sensitive feelers, advances and withdrawals, bids for leadership, alignment of forces, all take place as part of the 'hidden agenda' of interpersonal relations. One member may bring a complete solution along with him. His main preoccupation will be to watch for the right moment to slip it into the meeting. Its subsequent reception will partly be determined by the equilibrium processes at work in the committee. Or, another member may be sharply rebuked by someone in a dominant position to himself. His possible reaction will be to fall silent, contributing no remarks for the next ten or fifteen minutes. Once equilibrium has been established it proves very resistant to change, as is found in interaction between psychotherapists and patients over long series of sessions. For some combinations of people, equilibrium is very difficult or impossible, e.g., if all want to dominate, or one wants to be intimate and others want to be formal and distant. A manager should therefore study these equilibrium processes, since if he understands them he will be able to control the human situation more effectively. Since equilibrium is so resistant to change, while industry is in a state of constant change, the manager may well find it easier to effect changes by restructuring situations so that new equilibrium processes are forced to establish themselves, rather than to attempt to influence old behaviour patterns.

THE RULES AND STRUCTURE OF SOCIAL SITUATIONS

In any culture there are established rules about how interaction shall proceed in different situations, and between people in different relationships. Barker and Wright found 2,030 different situations in a small midwest town; going to church, going to the barber, etc.—each with its own rules. These rules cover (a) the kinds of behaviour which are suitable in the situation, and (b) the *structure* or sequence of events which must be followed, as in an interview or a church service. The rules and structure have developed during the history of the culture as acceptable ways of conducting different kinds of encounter.

Argyle and Little found that social interaction at work is in general rather different from behaviour at home or with friends, though it varies between manual and professional workers. Professional people report that they indulge in less gossip when at work than when at home or with friends, conversation is primarily about the task being performed, they are more polite, talk less about sex, are more concerned with their appearance, do not reveal their emotional states, attitudes to others, personal problems or ambitions, do not touch people, and behaviour is more formal. The pattern for manual workers is quite different. However, within the work situation there are different rules for specific situations. The selection interview for example has a number of rules, e.g., the interviewer and candidate sit down, are formally dressed and speak politely, the interviewer asks most of the questions, and takes notes, but does not ask personal questions which are irrelevant to the job. These situations also have a structure. The selection interview can be said to consist of the following stages: (1) Welcome, introductory chat, explanation of procedure, (2) acquiring information from the candidate, (3) supplying information in response to candidate's questions, (4) parting, comprising conclusion and farewell. Each stage has a structure of its own; for example, stage (2) has a series of sub-sections dealing with different phases of the candidate's experience or abilities, often in biographical order. Each of these sub-sections has a further structure, e.g., (1) open-ended question on the area in question, (2) reply, (3) follow-up question, (4) reply, (5) further follow-up question related to the last reply, etc., (6) interviewer summarises what he has learnt from this part of the interview and checks his conclusions with the candidate.

There are cross-cultural differences in the rules of social behaviour. It has been found that Arabs differ from Americans in general style of interaction, by orientating head-on, sitting or standing closer, touching each other, looking in the eye more of the time, and in talking louder. The rules for specific

31

situations, such as buying and selling, interviewing, etc., may be quite different, and there may be situations in one culture which simply do not exist in another.

Social skills and work

The social skills involved in work are somewhat different from the social skills used in other parts of everyday life. Although it is now realised that 'personality' is not constant in all situations, there are for any individual sets of situations in which he will behave in much the same way. These groupings of situations are much the same for people sharing the same cultural background. All work situations have something in common and are somewhat different from family situations, for example.

Some of the social skills used at work are relatively independent of the technology in which the individual operates. Examples are negotiation, discussion and committee work. For these skills, the model on page 26 applies. Other skills are affected by technology. For example in most supervisory or advisory relationships the performer does not do the work himself but makes sure that someone else does it. The model is shown in Fig. 2.2. Here the performer receives and must interpret feedback both from the task displays and from the subordinates' behaviour. He does not operate the task controls himself, but has to influence his subordinates to do so. He cannot do this unless he understands the task displays and the interaction between display and subordinate behaviour. This is a very simple example of a socio-technical system. In many work situations, social skills must be used in relation to a definite task and technological system, and an organisational setting, which to a large extent pre-programmes the relations between people. Some technical systems impose certain social arrangements; others can be operated by alternative socio-psychological systems which are each dependent on the technology. Until recently very little attention was paid by

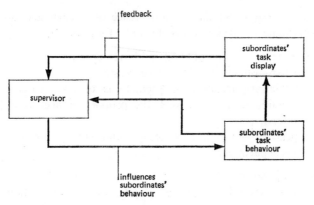

Fig. 2.2.

social scientists to the effects of technology on the social relations between workers. The main relationship envisaged was between a foreman and the individuals he supervised. In fact the matter is far more complex than that. When a worker has to deal with his job, and with other workers, he is carrying out a combination of a technical skill and a social skill.

Managers therefore need to understand the functioning of work-flow systems as a whole, so that they can deal with the social problems which they may engender. They also need to understand the general properties of social organisation. Both topics are discussed in Chapter 8.

The socially skilled person

We do not know whether or not there is a general disposition to be socially skilled, as there is to be intelligent. There may be no general factor of social competence running across all situations, or even all work situations. At present, it seems that social skill has to be recognised in relation to particular situations, or else recognised by its absence.

A person's competence at a manual skill is assessed by the results of his work, or by a test in which he does a standard

C

piece of work. Similarly, competence at a particular social skill can be assessed in terms of results; for example,

salesman—amount of goods sold over a period,
teacher—rate of examination successes,
interviewer—accuracy of predictions of later success of candidates (together with the proportion accepting job offers),
supervisor—output, absenteeism and labour turnover in his department.

Such measurements may not be easy: they may involve weighting several criteria, and may entail elaborate follow-up studies. However, this has been done for the skills mentioned, and for a number of others, and the social techniques used by the most competent performers have been discovered. The social competence of managers is more difficult to assess. Some studies have been undertaken, using indices such as ratings of departmental effectiveness by colleagues, and surveys of job satisfaction in the manager's department, but these are not entirely satisfactory. Part of the difficulty is that managers have to use a wide variety of social skills—interviewing, supervising, chairing meetings, etc.—and an individual may be better at some than others.

So one way of assessing social skills at work might be to rate an individual's performance in different situations and draw up a profile for him, as in Fig. 2.3. From these profiles it looks as though A would be better as a line manager, while B would be better as a personnel manager.

(Incidentally, a profile of this sort could have several uses. A manager might be able to observe and analyse his own social skills and draw his own skills profile. This would enable him to choose his own managerial career more effectively. It would reveal his strengths and weaknesses in these seven social skills areas, and indicate which he should try to improve by training and practice, in the ways discussed later in this book.)

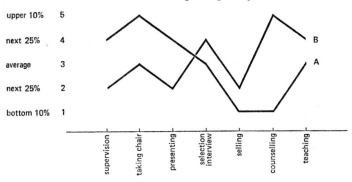

Fig. 2.3. Profiles of social skills

In addition to specific social skills, however, there is in most work situations a factor of everyday cooperation with members of the organisation. Here the criterion of success is less clear-cut; it often seems easier to recognise lack of social competence. We recognise social incompetence in a person who regularly annoys others, fails to establish friendly and cooperative relationships, and does not communicate clearly. We recognise it in someone who has difficulties in dealing with specific classes of person—women, Blacks, the upper classes, individual who suffers unduly from anxiety in social situations.

Several of the components of social skill which make a person effective or ineffective in general are probably:

(1) *Rewardingness.* A person's popularity is largely a function of his rewardingness to others—being helpful, kind, thoughtful, warm, easy to deal with. A rewarding person can also exert greater influence—since he is in a position to withdraw the rewards. Rewardingness is a key factor in social effectiveness in a wide variety of situations.

(2) *Perceptual sensitivity.* It is important for an interactor to be able to perceive accurately the emotional states and interpersonal attitudes of others, and also to judge moment-to-

35

moment reactions to what is being said or done—whether others are pleased or displeased, surprised, or disbelieving, agree or disagree.

(3) *Skill at synchronising*. The socially skilled person can deal rapidly and easily with a variety of interaction styles used by others. He can deal with people who talk too much or too little, are dominant or submissive, intelligent or unintelligent, etc. In some cases he is able to modify the behaviour of the other, e.g., putting an anxious person at ease, getting a silent person to talk more. He creates a smooth flow of conversation or other behaviour without interruptions, awkward pauses or misunderstanding.

(4) *Poise*. The skilled interactor is poised and at ease in social situations, and enjoys these situations. He does not suffer from continual anxiety, or worry about what others are thinking of him.

The acquisition of social skill

Social competence appears to be acquired during childhood and adolescence as a result of a variety of learning experiences. Children may learn by sheer trial and error which social techniques work and which do not. Social skills can be learnt by imitating others. Social skills can be taught by and assisted by verbal instruction (see Chapter 9) and by verbal commentary on behaviour. Parents usually provide some of this commentary as do teachers, and some schools are now introducing tuition specifically on social skills. School also provides a young person with his first experience of 'work' and of the social relationships that go with it. Certain basic components of the work personality appear to be laid down in the early school years: '. . . the ability to concentrate on a task for extended periods of time, the development of emotional response patterns to supervisory authority, the limits of cooperation and competition with peers, the meanings and values associated with work, the rewards and sanctions for achievement and non-achievement, the effects (both positive and negative) which become associated with being productive.'*

During adolescence there is experience of a wider variety of social roles and relationships. A new set of skills has to be acquired for dealing with the opposite sex. A different kind of relationship with parents and other adults is sought, and is often painfully acquired by what appears to be trial and error. This may lead to the odd and aggressive behaviour towards adults often shown by adolescents. They have their first experience of work proper in part-time and vacation jobs. The way young people are treated at work is usually rather different from the way they are treated at school, and there are rather different kinds of people to deal with: this is all further social-skill training. Many adolescents receive some experience of leadership through being captains of teams, or holding offices in clubs. On the other hand, young people receive little experience of many of the social skills needed at work, and these will have to be learned on the job, or on special training courses, as described in Chapter 9.

Further reading

A full account of the processes of social communication and inter-action can be found in:

Michael Argyle, *The Psychology of Interpersonal Behaviour* (2nd ed., Penguin Books, 1972)

A more detailed account of non-verbal signals can be found in:

M. L. Knapp, *Non-verbal Communication* (Rinehart and Winston, New York, 1972)

An account of the use of language in social situations can be found in:

Peter Robinson, *The Social Psychology of Language* (Penguin Books, 1972)

* W. S. Neff, *Work and Human Behavior* (Atherton Press, New York, 1968)

3
COMMUNICATION: SPEAKING AND WRITING

The last chapter discussed the range of verbal and non-verbal behaviours by which we influence each other in social encounters. It showed, however, that we do not all use all these behaviours equally skilfully. Some people are much better than others, both at using and also at perceiving nuances of behaviour; none of us is equally skilful in every social situation in which we have to cooperate. This is partly a function of our social experiences, which provide each person with somewhat different opportunities for learning. Most people in Britain have some opportunity of learning how to interact with parents and school teachers. Very few have mastered the behaviours required in Japanese tea-drinking ceremonies; not many more know the protocol associated with London livery company dinners.

Not only experience is involved, however. Mental abilities and emotional make-up affect how much we observe and learn and how careful we are to put what is learned into operation. It is not long before the individual is conditioned to pay particular attention to some aspects of his surroundings and to ignore others; some experiences he remembers for a short time and a selected few remain with him virtually permanently. In this chapter we briefly discuss the functions of perception, memory and attitudes and how they may affect social interaction. We also consider some of the ways in which communication between individuals is affected by the work environment. All social interaction has to be considered in the context of the personalities involved and the social and working groups in which they are operating. Finally, we discuss the implications of these influences for effective communication and the skills of speaking and writing.

Perception

A manager attends his annual golf club dinner. From all the sensory information involved in this experience, he pays special attention, let us suppose, to part of the menu, to one of the lady players, and to some casual discussion about rules of membership about which he holds strong opinions. Even before reaching home that night he has forgotten some of these events and others have grown in importance. Attitudes, perception and memory have all been involved in selecting and even modifying the experiences offered to him during the evening. When recounting the event, he gives his wife one version of what happened. Next day, he prepares another for his secretary and a third for colleagues in the managers' dining-room. For each story he chooses somewhat different facts and perhaps markedly different language and emphasis. Of course, this is not a situation where a manager might feel impelled to remember and record everything as accurately as possible. But many of the messages which he receives, and on which he bases his work, vary in tone, content and accuracy in a way not much different from the way in which he himself perceives the golf club dinner, and adapts the information he transmits. Messages are markedly affected by whether they come from friends, superiors, colleagues, rivals, subordinates, union representatives, buyers, suppliers or government officials—and also according to the recipient's position in the community and management hierarchy.

This process of selection and distortion is not random. We must select from the superabundance of experiences we receive. Since we cannot respond to them all we must decide, consciously or not, that some are important and others can be ignored. It may be a very difficult process to understand exactly what principles any individual is applying in his handling of experiences, but the general principles likely to apply to some extent to all of us are reasonably understood. As George Miller has pointed out: 'The inaccuracy of the testimony of eye-witnesses is well-known in legal psychology, but the distortions of testimony are not random. They follow naturally from the particular recoding that the witness used, and the particular recoding that he used depends upon his whole life history.'

What principles underlie the distorting or selecting processes in perception? Although the urge to 'make sense' of one's environment is not equally strong in everybody, only extremely disturbed people cease to show any interest in the 'meaning' of their experiences. The Roschach Inkblot Test is based upon this human proclivity. In this test the individual is presented with a series of cards showing ambiguous designs which were in fact developed originally by making inkblots and then folding over the paper. The individual is asked what he 'sees' on the cards. He usually responds by likening each design to a variety of objects, creatures or concepts. It is very rare for anyone to describe a design as simply an inkblot or to say they can see nothing in it. A good deal of training is required to interpret the responses to the Roschach Test, and the relationship of these interpretations to other criteria for assessing people is not well established. However, the important issue here is that since the designs are in fact meaningless *normal* responses to the cards provide a vivid demonstration of the creative, interpretative role of individual perception.

Reproductions of an ambiguous design, seen only briefly, consistently show a simplification of the original, a shift towards a 'better' design (e.g., more symmetrical, more probable) and a shift towards representation of a recognisable object. The perceivers 'makes sense' of the experience by ignoring 'irrelevant' details and increasingly assimilating it to something they already know. The same effect appears in repetition of stories or passing on items of information. The psychologist Wertheimer long ago pointed out that people will put meaning into a simple list of nouns. The list 'man, table, knife, cloth' easily relate to one concept, to which the word 'trolley' can be added without difficulty. But another concept is needed if the list is extended by the words—'surgeon, blood, anaesthetic'.

The distortions which information undergoes as a rumour develops were studied by Allport and Postman. They concluded that rumours are most rife when the information supplied is inadequate and/or ambiguous and people have a great need for the facts. They analysed wartime rumours and found that the few facts available were interpreted in ways which either comforted people ('The war will be over by Christmas') or confirmed, and so excused, the strong anxieties they were feeling ('Our losses are much worse than we have been told').

Perception is thus a dynamic activity, whereby the individual interprets to himself those parts of his environment which he selects for attention. A great many studies have been concerned with trying to determine how this selection occurs. Whether a person notices information presented to him depends on (1) the nature of the message, (2) his previous experience, (3) his current needs and interests.

Information is most readily perceived if it is both relevant to the individual's current needs and interests and confirms the views and attitudes he holds based on his previous experience. Information relevant to current needs but challenging established attitudes is attended to, but is likely to be rejected unless presented very persuasively. Information which either does not relate to the perceiver's present interests or challenges his views about them has to be presented very forcefully indeed if he is to take any notice. These effects are heightened the more strongly the individual is involved in his current task or preoccupied by current needs.

Forceful presentation may mean changing the kind of message (e.g., changing from notice board to radio announcement) or the intensity of the presentation. More noise or stronger colour will certainly attract attention to the message. These shock effects soon wear off, however. Once someone has accommodated to the higher level of stimulation, only another proportionate increase will impress him. The advertising industry wages a perpetual battle against this phenomenon.

Our preference for familiar undisturbing information is amply confirmed in studies of the audiences of mass media programmes. They show, hardly surprisingly, that people tend to select programmes that support their existing point of view and to avoid programmes, newspapers, etc., which state opinions which they find distasteful. This effect is particularly marked with people whose convictions are changing or who have only recently reached a decision on some issue. One study showed that people who had recently bought a new car spent most time looking at advertisements for the make they had bought rather than for competing makes. People with a well-established interest in a subject, on the other hand, will attend to all relevant information, whether or not it confirms their settled opinion.

One study analysed the amount of information absorbed by different groups of employees in a civilian department of a US Naval Ordnance Test Station. This showed that an average of 44 per cent of the items of information distributed by management was actually absorbed by employees. However, each group absorbed a rather higher percentage of those items which were particularly relevant to their own work. For example, 53 per cent of the engineers knew about engineering information brought back from a superior's trip to Washington, against 22 per cent of the administrative staff. These studies also show a sort of compound interest effect; interest in and knowledge of a subject encourages attention to relevant information, which in turn leads to greater knowledge and, generally, increased interest. Conversely, people remove themselves from situations where they are likely to encounter distasteful or frightening information. This is obvious in social situations where, given freedom of choice, people elect to be with others like themselves and to avoid those whose behaviour and opinions challenge their values.

Although working with another person generally tends to increase liking, it has been found that if people already strongly disliked each other, increasing contact between them simply served to strengthen their dislike. Frequent communication amongst staff at work was found to form an attraction or an irritation, according to the opinion each person held of the others. If a man values the contribution made by his colleagues he is glad to work with them and the values he shares with them are enhanced. However, being forced to work with those whom one does not value increases dislike, presumably because it reflects on one's self-esteem. This is analogous to being required to receive distasteful information, because it also is inimicable to the picture one has of oneself.

In laboratory experiments, people shown pictures of attractive, neutral or distasteful subjects have been found to take longer to recall the subject matter of pictures they disliked. An early experiment requiring people with pro- and anti-Communist sympathies to study pro- and anti-Communist literature, showed marked differences between the two groups, with each group assimilating more rapidly and forgetting more slowly the literature favourable to their established point of view. Conversely, they learned less of the unfavourable material and forgot it more rapidly. Certain posters have provided examples of people's handling of distasteful information presented to them in an open social situation. Posters depicting very vividly the horrors of, e.g., road accidents or lung cancer may become the subject of conversational jokes.

Such behaviour presents something of a puzzle. Although one may prefer to ignore, suppress or distort disturbing information, the information usually implies that action needs to be taken, on one's own behalf or on behalf of others. For example, it may be easier to assume, when redundancies are expected, that one will not oneself be amongst those leaving, but this easy device prevents one making any useful preparations for the future. Evidence that one is not popular with others can easily be distorted (most commonly into the formula that others are not worth speaking to). But this again prevents one from doing anything to make oneself more agreeable. Similarly, accidents do happen on the roads every day, with more or less serious implications, and cigarette smoking is conclusively linked with the risk of lung cancer. Ignoring this sort of information looks as though something has gone wrong with the primary instinct for self-preservation.

THE SOURCE OF INFORMATION

So far, we have considered factors in the message itself which influence perception. But the perceiver pays at least as much attention to the source of the information. A message from a junior or an incompetent, unattractive colleague is not attended to as carefully as one from a superior, a friend or someone highly respected. A message may come from top management, from the trade union representative, from the immediate work team or some professional association to which the manager belongs. He will have different views about all of these people and groups, and will accord them different degrees of trust and loyalty. These feelings will inevitably affect his reception of any information they provide.

A number of studies have shown how audiences respond to different types of speaker. The expert has an advantage in convincing them, intellectually, on an issue. Expertise is relied upon particularly when the listeners are struggling to assimilate unfamiliar or ambiguous information. They are convinced intellectually, partly because they rely upon the speaker's knowledge.

An attractive speaker, however, persuades people more easily, apparently because they respond to his attraction by adjusting their values to be more in tune with his. Attractiveness in a speaker derives from various sources. It may consist in his similarity with his audience—the values and interests he shares with them—or from his possession of attributes

44

(abilities, attainments, status, etc.) which they recognise as desirable whether or not these relate to his message. Thus an audience will decide, for example, how clever a speaker is, which is probably relevant, and will also decide that he is neat, sloppy, too fat, good looking, etc., etc., and a number of other things about him which are probably quite irrelevant. But they will judge him and respond to his message in terms of this total impression. In one experiment powerful communication was achieved by established experts who made small deliberate (irrelevant) mistakes, which apparently served to imply that although expert, they still shared with their audience an attractive human fallibility.

A speaker's power is the extent to which he is able to influence his audience's circumstances. Audiences tend to appear to comply with powerful figures but privately may not agree.

Other studies have compared the relative importance in attracting attention of the source of the message, its emotional appeal and its appeal to logic. A message may have emotional appeal because it links with the recipient's feelings, goals and values or simply because it generates pleasant feelings (warmth, humour, generosity, etc.). There is little difference between the power of emotion and of logic to attract attention, but what there is favours emotion. The influence of the source of the message is difficult to disentangle from either, since recipients can reasonably take into account the expertise of the source and will respond emotionally to his likeability.

The evidence is that we pay considerably more attention to someone addressing us in person than to a written communication from him. It has been found that a speech heard directly produced more opinion change and less hostility than the same speech delivered via a loudspeaker. One reason may simply be courtesy; we feel compelled to be more attentive, meeting someone face-to-face.

It may also be that the process of adaptation and adjustment to another's views acts more powerfully. The speaker himself can make a variety of spontaneous adjustments to

45

help this process which of course cannot be made in a written communication. He can alter his tone, wording and posture to strengthen his message and can respond appropriately to audience interest, puzzlement or irritation. These mutual adjustments occur to some extent even in phrases and voice tones used in telephone conversations. Simply to attract and hold attention, there seems no adequate substitution for direct personal communication.

The Acton Society Trust reached some depressing conclusions about the effects of quantities of information supplied to miners by the Coal Board management in the early 1950s. The information, principally stressing the need for higher output, came in pamphlets and magazines and even in a personal letter from the Prime Minister. But, as one Area General Manager said, '. . . nobody bothered to read it'. No questions were asked at the joint consultative meetings and nobody read the minutes of the meetings when they went up on the notice-board. Talking at Lodge meetings also proved ineffective because so few miners attended. 'This is really our major difficulty—how to put the information across and how to rid the minds of the men of misconceptions.' One may speculate that neither the message itself nor its source met the conditions for attracting this audience's attention. Methods of communication in the coal industry were subsequently made much more direct and personal and radically improved.

T. H. Higham undertook a study of rumours and was able to demonstrate the expected distortions of information. During the course of the study, however, he happened to give a student some information relevant to examination standards. This particular piece of information was rapidly transmitted with marked accuracy to every member of quite a large student group. Why? In the first place, the information was of very considerable interest to all the recipients. Secondly, it was highly advantageous to them. Thirdly, the information was apparently given inadvertently, or certainly not as a special matter for instruction. It appeared as 'pure' information, not with any biased intent. Finally, it came as a personal message from a highly respected source.

The source of information is undoubtedly very influential in attracting and holding attention whatever the type of message. However, it seems that the source is rather less important when it comes to ensuring that a message is remembered, although we also know that the expert source is remembered longest, the attractive source next and the powerful source least. A number of experiments have compared the memorability of information from sources recognised as either credible or biased. Whilst the same message certainly roused favourable or unfavourable reactions according to source, these reactions wore off in a few weeks. It seemed that audiences, regardless of their original views of the speaker, had shifted opinions by about the same amount. These experiments suggest that whether an audience is prepared to accept or to reject a speaker, in the end the facts and opinions he conveys come to be assimilated and to modify or consolidate opinions in much the same way.

These experiments, however, have all been conducted on speeches. When talk is followed or largely replaced by discussion, the results are different. Wherever the audience becomes involved in the subject, to the extent of asking questions and relating its implications to their own situation, the amount of information remembered and the degree to which attitudes change are both markedly increased. In these circumstances, it seems reasonable to assume that the audience's opinion of the speaker is very important, not just because it affects how much attention he commands but also because it makes easier the development of discussion and participation which in turn affect remembering.

CONVEYING COMPLEX AND ALARMING INFORMATION

It is clear that special problems attend the tasks of conveying complex and ambiguous information and of conveying alarming information. Complexity and ambiguity are best tackled by ensuring that the message is conveyed by authoritative and attractive sources in accordance with modern teaching principles (see below). There seem to be two conditions which enable people to receive unpleasant information. The first is that it should not be presented in too sudden or alarming a fashion. People will attend to mildly threatening news and can gradually assimilate the appalling. The second condition is that people have an opportunity to improve matters. Along with the information, with its consequences for them, they are given the practical steps they can take to offset these effects. The increasing practice of giving long-term notice of redundancy, combined with practical help in finding new employment, meets these conditions.

INDIVIDUAL DIFFERENCES IN PERCEPTION

These general observations on the function of perception have been supplemented by work on individual differences. Although most people need to 'make sense' of their environment, there are some established differences in the way they set about it. Cohen, summarising work on ways of thinking, concludes that people differ considerably in their need to acquire knowledge, from those who are content to remain ignorant to those with a passion to know all they can possibly absorb. People also appear to differ in the strength of their need for cognitive clarity. People in whom this need is marked are concerned with the meaningfulness of all aspects of their experience. They will start work on a laboratory puzzle even before being told why it is important. Those with less need may eventually work as effectively but not until the possible value of the solution has been explained to them.

Other studies have divided people into 'sharpeners' and 'levellers'. Sharpeners look for distinguishing details in any new problem and seize on every cue that may help them to understand an ambiguous situation. Levellers dislike ambiguity and turn their attention away from any details which make the situation confusing. People who most readily accept new information are sharpeners with a high need for cognitive clarity.

People also vary in their readiness to be persuaded. This quality is related to age and sex. Children around nine years old tend to be highly persuasable and women tend to be more persuasable than men. However, there is no consistent link between persuasability and intelligence. McGuire suggests this is because persuasability seems to have two elements, one of which seems likely to relate to limited ability and the other to high. To be persuaded, the recipient must in the first place be perceptive and the more able are capable of receiving greater amounts of more complicated information than the less able. But in addition to noticing and understanding the information, the recipient must be persuaded by it. Here the more able are less affected than the limited because they can think up better counter arguments.

ATTRACTING AND HOLDING ATTENTION

There are a number of lessons for a manager in these studies. For instance, however considerable his personal skills of presentation, a manager is unlikely to attract and hold attention if he cannot relate his message to the known interests and needs of the people he is addressing.

A number of experiments have compared the effects of (1) giving information and then explaining its implications for the hearer, against (2) explaining how the hearer may be affected and then giving the relevant information. Although some people pay equal attention to the information in either circumstance, many attend only when the reasons for paying attention have been given. Managers should therefore be careful to show wherever possible that their message relates to attainment of the individual's desired objectives or can strengthen his self-esteem. It is always worth telling people, for instance, that any subject they are required to study has been mastered and found valuable by some person they are likely to admire or some group with which they can identify.

Particular effort is needed to relate unfamiliar material to the audience's established interests. Imaginative linking, together with a forceful and lively presentation, is required to help most audiences if they are to sustain for any time the effort of attending to new information. Even then, new concepts should be introduced sparsely, so as to allow for the inevitable fluctuations and strain on attention which they introduce.

All information is, of course, received in competition with other preoccupations. Well-designed training programmes allow, amongst other things, for course members' varying attention before and after meals, concern over travel arrangements and so forth.

SELF-PRESENTATION

The studies make it clear that managers cannot safely ignore the question of self-presentation. Personal communication is preferable to written, even though both may be needed (see below). It is also important for the presenter to appear as expert and as likeable as possible.

Clients, buyers, suppliers or government officials need reassurance that they are hearing from the best person to inform them about the particular case. Some self-presentation can be done in conversation, not in the sense of baldly stating one's qualifications, but showing unobtrusively that one has relevant knowledge or experience. Sometimes a letter of introduction from a senior person can help; it should mention the manager's relevant expertise. In other circumstances a handout supplying title or qualifications may be appropriate. Speakers can usually rely on the chairman's introduction to explain to the audience why they may be worth hearing.

Expertise is also conveyed by manner, above all by a consistent standard of competence and confidence in presenting the facts. Audiences are sharply alert to any faltering in this role, especially when they are using (as they often must) an estimate of the speaker's calibre to help in evaluating the facts he supplies.

Goffman describes how professional people often play a role and put on a performance. The situation is that the competent are rewarded by audience trust and respect, and the incompetent will gain trust and respect insofar as they can consistently pretend to it.

In addition to supplying his credentials, the manager can be careful to state any important values, attitudes or interests which he or his organisation shares with his audience. ('We are as concerned as you are to reduce costs. . . .' 'We are agreed, I know, that this market could be considerably developed. . . .') Simply a skilful use of pronouns can build solidarity, e.g. using 'we' instead of 'you' and 'I'.

Much is conveyed by dress and appearance and a manner which indicates standards mutually shared. Manner will also indicate the relationship the manager wishes to develop. A mixture of independent assurance (with regard to the facts) and friendly sympathy (with regard to their application to the clients' circumstances) often seems appropriate.

The physical layout of the room is also important. Speakers, instructors and presenters should make every effort to see any room in which they will work beforehand, and make any adjustments (e.g. in the arrangement of tables and chairs) likely to foster the desired relationship.

Implications for written communications

Accepting that personal communication is particularly valuable in attracting and holding attention, it remains true that the manager who must communicate in writing can usefully follow these same rules to some extent. Youthful professional people, submitting scientific papers, benefit from the stated support of their professors; unknown book authors are wise to acquire a preface written by someone eminent in their field. A manager writing a report should make sure that any justification for his writing on the subject, rather than anyone else, is clearly stated.

Similarly, it is usually possible, in all but highly formal documents, to include some phrase indicating common interests with the reader, or simply warmth and interest. Even manner and appearance can be translated to some extent into writing, the first by individual style and the second by the company's standard of letterhead, layout, typography, etc.

Memory

Supposing that the information the manager wishes to convey has been noticed and received without too much immediate distortion, the next risk is that it may be very rapidly forgotten. There seem to be two sorts of memory—short-term and long-term—and they operate in somewhat different ways. Most of us can acquire a limited amount of information for short-term use (and it seems that very few people can improve on that span regardless of training). However, the short-term memory store is quite small and new information is added to it only at the expense of material already there. Something else has to be pushed out.

It is as though a warehouseman were to make room for newly delivered goods simply by pushing some of the older stock out of a back door into the street. Much of what is pushed out of the short-term memory does metaphorically go into the street. It deteriorates and is lost. But a few items are pushed through another door. They are somehow selected to go into the long-term memory store. Once an item is in the long-term memory it appears to be there more or less permanently. This does not mean that is is always available for instant recall. The interference of new ideas and experiences prevents our using much of the information which we acquired, for example, in earlier years. But the information appears not to decay, as it would in the short-term memory, and it can be brought to the surface, e.g. with the help of drugs or hypnosis. In old age short-term memory may deteriorate badly, but that which was stored in the long-term memory remains. So is produced the phenomenon in which an old person cannot recall where he left his spectacles a few seconds ago, but can describe in intimate detail some event from his childhood.

How material is selected to go into the long-term memory is not fully understood. Broadbent has speculated on a special mental faculty which 'recognises' material in the short-term memory as having special significance. Some of the problems which older people have in acquiring new information seem to relate to the problem of altering this monitor's recognition of what is significant. An analogy would be with a secretary who knew all her bosses' activities and had developed an appropriate filing system. She would sort the day's mail and doubtless jettison a good deal, but file the significant material appropriately. Initally it would be a small matter to add new files or even revise the system. But considerable inconvenience and temporary inefficiency could be involved in revising a large, well-established system. The secretary would have a strong interest in maintaining the existing arrangement, to the extent of filing material inappropriately rather than attempt a reorganisation. Adults do, in fact, experience particular difficulty in acquiring accurately any information which is somewhat like other material with which they are already familiar.

However, it can reasonably be assumed that communications have a better chance of entering most people's long-term memories if they relate to general motives which most people hope to satisfy at work. The chances are further increased, one must suppose, if the communication can be more closely related to the particular drives and interests which are known to prevail within a group or with an individual. Some methods of training discussed below help memory by allowing the individual to select and assimilate the information he needs.

It may also be recognised that an individual's ability to learn is fostered by working in a generally stimulating environment. There is much evidence that higher creatures are impelled by general curiosity to explore their surroundings, without motivation from specific drives such as hunger. Thus it might be argued that the best learning situation would simply be one in which the individual was presented with a succession of relevant and challenging problems. Few senior managers have difficulty in ensuring this sort of environment for themselves and many of the most promising developments in management training (see below) are attempts to provide the same sort of relevant challenges to more junior people.

Within these general observations, however, a number of rules can usefully be followed to encourage people to remember:

REWARDS AND PUNISHMENTS

People learn little when their efforts receive neither reward nor punishment. In general, though there are some personality differences in this, they learn best when rewarded for achievement and rather less effectively when punished for failure. Both reward and punishment need to follow performance promptly and precisely.

Rewards for successful performance make for more effective learning than punishments for failure apparently because:

(1) punishment may lead the trainee to perceive learning as a generally disagreeable experience;

(2) at best, punishment serves to define areas of failure and examples of negative behaviour. But it is more difficult to learn from a negative concept than from a positive.

Maximally effective learning, however, appears to occur when rewards are consistently given for the desired performance but are not invariably earned. It seems there must be challenge (i.e. some risk of failure) in the learning task to sustain motivation. Perhaps self-esteem suffers if one is asked to learn tasks which seem 'too easy'.

Intrinsic rewards are likely to be more effective than extrinisc. The rewards of learning to play the piano, ride a bicycle or drive a car are intrinsic; once students have reached some level of proficiency they will practise these skills for their own sake. Extrinsic incentives may be needed, however, to start them off; a punishment for failing, or a prize for passing the driving test, might serve the purpose. Well-designed instructions, e.g. for operating a machine or a procedure should bring the intrinsic reward of performing correctly. Programmed courses have failed to teach only where the steps have appeared to the student too trivial for him to pursue conscientiously; part of the skill of effective programming is to select units of information sufficient to provide the intended student with some mental challenge and the intrinsic motivation this involves.

PROVIDING A FRAMEWORK

Most studies of learning show that people do best if they can initially acquire a general picture of the subject (or a general notion of the skill) which they can subsequently enrich and elaborate. As an example, someone attempting to learn a poem would probably do better in the end, though not initially, if he each time read through and tried to recite the entire poem. This process would gradually fix the whole pattern of the poem in his mind and he would be spared the task of building a framework within which to anchor each verse, whilst also struggling to learn his words. It is easy for managers and trainers to forget the framework of concepts which they themselves have come to take for granted, but without which much of their communication may seem meaningless.

A major difficulty in writing a layman's handbook on any technical subject is to make explicit in the script all the information which is entirely self-evident to the design and production staff involved. A country housewife once wrote angrily to the manufacturers on the inadequacy of her new cooker. The engineer sent to investigate could find nothing wrong. At last they agreed that he should watch her step-by-step through the cooking of some item, which she did with the aid of the handbook. Its limitation as a guide to good cookery soon appeared. The book did not explain that, once a dish was put in the oven, the oven door should be shut.

A similar problem certainly underlies some of the failures of young employees to master a job in the time their seniors consider reasonable. Conversely, one of various reasons for the success of properly designed programmed learning courses is the care that goes into ensuring that all items essential to understanding the subject are included in logical sequence.

SPACED LEARNING

In general, people learn less when working in a concentrated burst than when study periods are spaced. Learning periods need to be interspersed with periods of other activities—perhaps listening to more familiar information, perhaps discussing or applying what has been learned. In written material, the reader is helped to understand new concepts if they are introduced sparingly and each one discussed and elaborated and linked to more familiar ideas.

REPETITION

Even when the student seems to have grasped the issue, it is useful to repeat important information throughout a course or presentation. To prevent boredom it must of course be offered in a different context, or in some way which shows its relevance to a new situation. Overlearning of central issues ensures that they become habitual modes of thought or behaviour.

GROUPING INFORMATION

Experiments on perception and hearing have shown that human powers of discrimination cannot extend beyond a very small range of facts or experiences. For example, the ability to learn a new number drops off dramatically if the number contains more than seven or eight digits. Our current all-digit telephone numbers are on the verge of this outside limit. We deal with this difficulty by dividing the material we have to learn into 'meaningful' groups, and treating each group as an item. We put things into one group because they are near to each other, or because they are similar or because they have similar functions. Anyone who can impose this sort of order on his material from the outset does a good deal to help ensure that his message will be remembered.

Occasionally, material defies 'meaningful' interpretation and has simply to be acquired by rote. In this situation, mnemonics and rhymes can help. There is no logic in the number of days in our calendar months but at least the rhyme 'Thirty days hath September . . .' ensures that every child knows at an early age what that number is.

Application to verbal and written communication

If these rules are put together they begin to indicate the reasons for the structure advocated for an effective talk or presentation, and to show similarity between this structure and the plan adhered to in well-written reports and scientific papers.

THE PLAN OF A TALK

The audience or reader must first be motivated to pay attention. A good speaker, instructor or presenter opens his subject by answering the audience's question:

What is the problem?
How does it concern us?
Why should we attend to it?
Why should it interest us?

Next, he sets out the scope of the subject with an indication of the different points to be covered in detail. The points follow, grouped and reduced to an essential minimum. Under each, the theoretical concept or principal is given, its relation to the audience's interest may be restated and the theory illustrated by example. In conclusion, he repeats the essential message reinforced with the most important of his logical and persuasive arguments, again linked to the audience's interest.

THE STRUCTURE OF A REPORT

How does such a pattern compare with the structure of a report, apparently an entirely different type of communication? A report is usually a commissioned document required from an expert in the subject by a superior who has to take a decision about it. The central problem for the report writer is to leave his reader as informed as he is himself on the relevant issues, but with a mind left free to consider objectively the various possible courses of action. The writer is entitled (often required) to recommend one of the possible courses of action; but he is expected to argue his case plainly. He has to convince if he can by logic—not to persuade the reader and certainly not to mislead him (e.g. by omission or distortion of any uncomfortable relevant information).

Such ends are achieved largely by scrupulous adherence to a structure or plan of presentation which divides facts from comments and indicates all potential sources of bias. These are the essential features of any document which attempts to present information objectively. Scientific papers follow the same structure; the quality press is distinguished from the popular partly by its more careful distinction between fact and opinion and by more references to specific sources of information.

Potential sources of bias in any document or oral presentation of facts are: the writer/presenter himself (his personality; his own values and opinions); the writer/presenter's role in relation to his reader/audience (subordinate, adviser, possibly competitor); the way in which information was collected; the constraints of time, money, resources, etc., within which the facts were gathered; the considerations applied in analysing the facts.

These potential sources of bias are ineradicable in human communication. But the structure of a good report ensures that at least they are recorded. The reader knows who is writing to whom, why and in what circumstances. The description of the method of investigation, the appendices and the bibliography tell him about any limitations in collecting information. The considerations applying in analysing the facts are clearly stated.

There are also stylistic conventions in report writing that attempt to reduce the influence of the writer's personality. Sentences are commonly written impersonally 'a random sample of a hundred customers was visited', not 'I visited . . .' This style directs attention to the subject matter and away from the reporter. The language is expected to be factual and objective, with a minimum of adjectives and adverbs—not, 'We suffered appalling losses on exports . . .', but 'Profits from exports fell by 80 per cent . . .'

With all these distinctions, a report of any length is likely to include the following sections, usually in this order:

(1) title, author, intended reader(s);

(2) terms of reference (authorisation and purpose);

(3) summary (covering main points in all other sections and constituting a birds-eye view);

(4) background history/review (of relevant research prior to current investigation);

(5) method of investigation;
(6) findings (a) general or major, (b) special or minor;
(7) analysis of findings (including criteria applied);
(8) discussion/conclusions;
(9) recommendations.

In addition, it may have appendices but these are reserved for relevant but detailed information liable to distract from the main theme of the report.

The prime purpose of this structure is to encourage the reader to objective thought. But in fact it bears a resemblance to the structure followed by the persuader or instructor. It provides motivation by answering at the outset questions about the problem and why the appropriate reader should be interested. It supplies an initial survey of the subject, so that the reader does not subsequently have the double task of acquiring specific information whilst attempting to fit it into a general plan. It ensures that the most important information appears two or three times in different sections (e.g. in the Summary, the Findings and perhaps the Analysis and Recommendations). Finally, the important information is likely to be presented in a variety of verbal and visual forms.

Application to training

Various new developments in training take into account these and other findings on learning. A consideration of three new systems of training may show the common elements in the principles which they apply.

PROGRAMMED INSTRUCTION

This reduces the difference in learning performance between different levels of intellectual ability partly because it provides a firm framework for learning. The effort of learning to learn is much less with a programmed text than with a standard textbook. Another reason for the effectiveness of programmed learning is that while all students work through the same programme, each student works at his own pace. A third is that, although feedback is prompt and precise, only the student need know of his own successes and failures. Older people in general, and probably the less able in particular, become especially discouraged if their early failures to master a subject occur in public.

THE 'DISCOVERY' METHOD OF LEARNING

This was developed by Belbin from his extensive studies of the learning difficulties of older people. In this method, the learning task is presented to the trainee as a series of problems which he is required to solve for himself. For example, he might have to learn how to start and operate a machine. The whole task may be subdivided by the trainer into a series of small problems which the trainee can be set in sequence. The handles and parts which he should manipulate to solve each problem are clearly indicated. Within this carefully protected situation, the trainee is allowed to teach himself and the trainer's role is confined to giving information as required and providing friendly encouragement.

The discovery method has produced results superior to more traditional training methods in various experiments. The method seems to build upon those habits of learning which are likely to be maintained by everyone. In ordinary life, we are often required to work empirically towards the solution of problems. The discovery method makes the same demands, but eliminates the waste and hazards of unguided exploration.

TARGET SETTING

Some parallels can be drawn between the discovery method and the technique of target setting. This technique was not developed to help the learning processes of less able people. Indeed, it is virtually always applied to managerial work and tends to be accepted most readily by younger and more able

61

managers. But target setting defines the tasks the manager faces, the standards he should achieve and the conditions within which he must operate. Ideally, the target is within the manager's capacity but still presents him with a challenge. He works out for himself how best to achieve it and thus learns within the presumably safe boundaries of discretion established with his superior.

Some experiments on problem-solving have indicated the influence of the exact wording of instructions upon the student's performance. In one experiment, a difference in the originality of responses appeared according to whether the student was asked simply to solve the problem or to find an original solution. In another, different phrases used to help students memorise material were found to relate to the ease with which they subsequently solved different sorts of problem. These detailed experiments again reaffirm the importance of directing attention precisely and setting clear objectives, all marked features of successful modern training methods.

Attitudes

Experimental work, such as has been quoted, has indicated some of the ways in which perception and memory work. What is perceived or remembered, however, is governed by each individual's prevailing values, judgements, attitudes. Some consideration of the function of attitudes and how they develop may indicate how they are likely to affect communication between the individual and his fellows. Attitudes have the following functions:

(1) They serve as a short cut for handling new experiences and information. Particularly in the absence of full understanding or a new or complex or ambiguous issue, the individual relies on his established attitudes as a basis for making a judgement about it.

(2) They gain him acceptance in a particular group, to

define him as a member of, e.g., a particular nation, relation, class, political party, etc. He asserts his membership by holding values in common with the group and cannot greatly deviate from these values without losing membership and the security it brings.

(3) They help the individual to express his needs and interests and to define his self-image.

(4) They may justify his behaviour in dealing with a particular environment. Thus a child's need to come to terms with a punitive, powerful father may form the basis of an authoritarian attitude in later life.

Most important attitudes are formed gradually from a total life experience. They have some genetic base, in that they are affected by innate endowments—the individual's intelligence and stability, the amount of aggression he brings to life, his tendency to be influenced. They also appear to be modified by age, so that within a culture certain attitudes are typical of most children of the same age or most adolescents. They may be modified by illness or drugs. They tend to be most strongly held and protected from 'damaging' influences when they are newly formed.

A few adult attitudes appear to relate unduly to a limited number of powerful traumatic incidents, particularly any experienced in early childhood. Attitudes formed in this way, however, are usually inadequate for handling later experience and may render their possessor a candidate for psychotherapy. The function of attitudes is so important that it is not surprising they are not easily changed. Psychotherapy, which attempts to alter attitudes damaging to the individual, is a slow and uncertain process.

CHANGING ATTITUDES

A major function of attitudes is to determine the way in which an individual interacts with other people. Brainwashing works—insofar as it does—by destroying the bases on which the individual expects to gain acceptance from other people. In our society, a more acceptable way of modifying attitudes is through group participation. Many experiments in management training have the objective of modifying individual attitudes—most usually, perhaps, in the direction of increasing tolerance. The individual is to be enabled to receive more points of view or a greater range of facts than his attitudes so far have permitted him. The evidence is that the more active a part the individual can take in the whole process of persuasion or training, the more effective that process is likely to be.

If, for example, an audience hears one side of an issue and its members are then asked publicly to state their own opinions, this act alone is enough to increase resistance to hearing another point of view. In one experiment, students were asked either to prepare and deliver a talk on a subject with which they disagreed, or else simply to listen to a speech on the subject. The speech-givers—who had of course undertaken the double task of both preparing and delivering their talk—changed their views markedly more than those who only listened. There was also a positive relationship between the amount of change in the person giving the speech and the ingenuity and inventiveness demonstrated. In another experiment, people with known anti-Negro sympathies were asked either to watch or to act the role of a Negro going into a previously all-white neighbourhood. Control subjects did not alter their opinions; observers altered somewhat and role players most of all.

It seems that commitment, action and role-playing all help imagination and understanding of another's point of view. Even requiring students to recall information supplied, scarcely a participative teaching method, provides enough active response to improve learning. The only experiments where these effects did not occur have concerned highly distasteful roles which the player was paid to perform. In these circumstances, students who were offered very little money either declined the roles, or took them and changed their point of view. But students offered large sums took the money, played the roles and did not change their view. Apparently the larger sum of money seemed to justify the task and to permit its being performed without involvement. Discussion can produce considerable changes in attitude and behaviour provided the subject discussed is interesting and important to the student and has obvious implications for his everyday life.

An increasing number of courses in skills and techniques of management now rely on this form of instruction and may include very little direct instruction. Instead the course organisers are likely to design tasks for the students, from which the students themselves can proceed to deduce the principles and establish the skills involved in the subject. In these teaching methods attention, memory and attitudes are engaged together.

Implications for instructing and making presentations

Participation is undoubtedly the most efficacious way of encouraging people to reconsider their outlook. They are also, however, significantly more likely to accept new information or new points of view if the presenter follows some simple rules:

(1) State both sides of the case when presenting controversial information. Stating one side of the case only is effective with audiences of limited ability or education, with people who cannot be reached with counter-propaganda and with people who already agree with the speaker. But if we assume that there are few important issues where people living in a democracy can be protected from hearing opposing points of view, then the manager would do better to state both sides.

An effective pattern for a persuasive argument seems to be: show how the proposed action or viewpoint relates to the audience's needs and interests; state the opposing point of

E   65 view and give the objections to it; reaffirm the value of the proposed viewpoint.

(2) Give good news before bad. This is presumably because the bad news provokes resistance, but a piece of cheering information is welcomed. The audience remains attentive and thus hears the bad news that follows.

(3) Give major and significant arguments before the minor and be ready to repeat the major issue in conclusion. At the beginning, attention is fresh. At the end, the brain rests and last impressions are consolidated.

(4) State conclusions explicitly. In one study when the conclusions were explicitly stated, twice as many people changed their opinion in the direction indicated by the communicator as did when the conclusions were not drawn. This and many other experiments are summarised by Cohen. It seems that conclusions should be drawn increasingly carefully the more complex the issue, the less intelligent the audience and the more remote the subject from the audience's immediate interests.

Attitudes and the work hierarchy

This is a special aspect of the effect of attitudes upon social interaction. Working in a large organisation affects communication in a number of ways, a good deal because people's attitudes to each other are confused by their attitudes towards work roles. Paul Pigors pointed out that communications are varied in speaking to a person according to what he is—his organisational function in line management; where he is—at the top, middle or bottom of the hierarchy; and who he is—either as a person or as a member of a special interest group.

Moreover, there are practical difficulties in the way of effective communication from subordinate to superior. For a start, subordinates have fewer facilities for communication than do their superiors. Management rather than workers have the help of secretaries, duplicating facilities and the inter-com. Additionally, managers probably command greater linguistic and social skill. Then information coming from a lower level in the organisation may have to gain the attention of someone with a wide range of responsibilities, to whom it can appear parochial. Finally, much upward information, e.g. failure to meet a production requirement, machine-breakdown, sickness, is, if accurate, quite likely to mean extra demands on the superior. Too many accurate messages of this sort, coming from one person, may lead a senior to transfer his irritation from the problem to their transmitter. Here attitudes are involved rather than practicalities. Ambitious subordinates perceive this difficulty very clearly. One study showed that middle managers with the strongest aspirations towards promotion in the company communicated least accurately with their superiors.

Another study of patterns of communication in a medium-sized US government agency showed that people preferred to communicate with others likely to have the information they needed and likely to make them feel secure. The general effect was that people preferred to talk to those senior to themselves. But this did not mean that they wished to communicate disagreeable information. It was also a general rule in the agency that people communicated information in ways likely to improve their own position.

In the same vein, large numbers of valuable suggestions coming from the shop floor may constitute an unwelcome reflection on management standards. In one factory currently going through a phase of major removal and reorganisation, both a system of consultation and a suggestion scheme were turned down by management, precisely on these grounds: 'They'll think of hundreds of things we ought to be doing and it will just stir up discontent.'

In all, a good many barriers may have to be overcome in upward communication in an organisation. Moreover, even when the news is reasonably accurately received it often appears to be ignored. A matter which is urgent at factory or office level may be found to involve principles and precedents which demand careful discussions amongst senior people, who thus seem to be doing nothing about it. Perhaps the greatest deterrent of all in the development of upward communication is the feeling that it brings no results. Many a strike leader, official and unofficial, has claimed that the strike became necessary because orthodox communications went unanswered.

ENCOURAGING UPWARD COMMUNICATION

To overcome these problems, the Industrial Society advocates regular (perhaps monthly) briefing sessions in which groups of not more than eighteen employees meet their immediate boss, so that he can directly pass on management information and ensure that instructions, changes, etc., are explained and understood. Planty and McHaver advocate supervisors' clubs which, though primarily social, effectively bring supervisors together and are likely to produce exchange of work information. They also suggest that managers might prepare a list of items on which they would expect subordinates to keep them informed, and check that they have received the information and that they have heard from everybody. They point out the potential of the appraisal interview for encouraging upward communication and commend suggestion schemes and attitude surveys for the same reason. A democratic style of leadership, as discussed in Chapter 7, also helps improve upward communication.

STRATEGIC ROLES IN COMMUNICATION

In addition to this general problem, various studies have shown that certain positions and functions tend to be favoured or handicapped in receiving information, whether formally or through the grapevine. Staff people are often better informed than line managers (their job requires this and they are more mobile). Those working in geographically remote places, employees of low status and people whose work is unremittingly demanding, all tend to be left out of the communication system. Belonging to a small work group also affects communication with an individual in various ways. Depending on the group's working circumstances and relation to other working groups, he may receive information rapidly or be effectively barred from almost all outside influences. The group may determine how and when he receives information and what interpretation he puts upon it.

A superior's communications are received differently by a member of a united working group from the way in which they are received by a subordinate working on his own. Membership of a united group of peers gives security and a set of values by which to judge the superior's instructions. There is more freedom to argue. Long-established groups are likely to have very high morale and firmly established values and modes of interaction. Any newcomer to such a group is under great pressure to conform and will probably himself work hard to acquire the group's standards. Once he becomes established, however, it seems that he will attract a consistent amount of communication. If Group Member A addresses 25 per cent of his remarks to B, then C and D are likely to do the same.

However a group is run, it is fairly sure to have one or two recognised leaders. From the point of view of communication, their significance is that they are usually freer than the rest of the group to consider and adopt new ideas. They also hold the respect of the group so that any messages they transmit are attended to. Several studies have shown the influence throughout a group of a few influential personalities. In one study all the doctors in a given community were interviewed, records of their prescriptions were examined, and the social and professional patterns of interaction amongst them were studied. It was found that the doctors with the richest interaction with others were the most up-to-date with their treatments and felt happiest about trying new methods.

The social groups each contained one or two pioneers and once a pioneer had adopted a new treatment, about 50 per cent of the members of his medial clique would follow suit within a few days.

David traced items of information known to different members of management in one small company back to their source. He discovered that the grapevine depended heavily upon a few people who would pass on the information. One problem was known to 68 per cent of the executives, but only 20 per cent had actually passed it on. Only about six people, out of the total of sixty-seven managers, regularly passed on information to more than two other people. They selected the information to transmit, particularly passing on information relating to the job functions which interested them and to the people they knew socially. Davis calls them liaison officers and concludes that management could best improve communications by increasing the number of people willing to liaise.

Mass media programmes are found to have an indirect effect through the medium of opinion leaders. These are the trusted and informed members of a community group who tend to study the media and whose opinions are generally valued. When they transmit information it is absorbed because they are personally respected, because they can adjust the information to local and particular cases and because they can immediately reward agreement (e.g. by showing their approval).

It is through their leaders, in particular, that primary groups develop their relationship to the larger organisation. The famous Hawthorne experiments made everyone aware of how a strong group could defeat management's objectives (e.g. in controlling group output). In other situations, the group's acceptance of the values of the larger organisation can spur its members to exceptionally high performance. Towards the end of World War II, German soldiers continued to fight bitterly when the army was virtually defeated, because of their loyalty to their immediate fighting group. Thus a manager needs to take special pains to ensure that the opinion leaders in any group he controls are kept informed and that, as far as possible, these leaders are helped to see their own and their group's objectives as being furthered by achieving the aims of the larger organisation.

Choice of media

One or two points have become clear by now, as regards choice of media. Firstly, the message delivered in person has a great advantage over the written message in attracting and holding attention. Secondly, important and complex issues which require objective study must be written down. They also need to be carefully written according to a prescribed structure to enable the reader to consider their contents objectively. Thirdly, provided those concerned are personally affected by the issues at stake, participation is a powerful means of encouraging attitude change.

What other information can guide the manager in his choice of means for making a case or instructing staff? One experiment compared the effectiveness of ways of conveying information to groups of students, of employees in a small plastics manufacturing company and of office staff. The methods used were oral, oral and written, written only, bulletin board and grapevine. Results were measured in terms of correct answers to test questions. The information conveyed was relevant to each group, but unlikely to interest them greatly. For example, the employees of the plastics firm were given details of the company insurance scheme—information which was already available, though not generally studied with care, in the employee handbook.

The results showed that with all groups the combination of oral and written was the most successful, followed by oral only, then written only, then bulletin board. Last came the grapevine with results no better than chance. However, another finding was that amongst employed groups employees who had been with their firm for more than a year scored better than newcomers, regardless of methods used. Studies of audiences and readership for the mass media have shown that there is a positive correlation between level of education and reliance on the printed word. The less educated rely on oral and picture media. Other studies showed that the mass media preach to the converted, and also to the casual listener, with uncommitted views, who might watch a programme inadvertently.

Implications for instructing and communicating information

These and similar studies tend to confirm the inference that any communication has most chance of being noticed, understood and remembered if, in addition to following the rules outlined above, the manager presents his information in as many forms as possible. Presentations should include visual aids, such as charts, graphs and models, and written material. The major issues requiring decision can be summarised in a handout; or tables can be issued which give the detailed figures on which a graph is based. It is also useful to vary the oral presentation, e.g., by introducing tape recordings, a second speaker, etc.

Offering a variety of channels whereby the message can reach the mind also gives individuals freedom of choice in how they learn. They can decide from which source to absorb the information, and even to a limited extent at what pace they will proceed. Even programmed courses are not the answer to all problems, because they cannot replace all elements in the optimal teaching situation. They become fully effective when part of a total training programme which can include discussion, practical work with guidance, and so forth.

Other findings suggest that a campaign spread over time can be expected to foster and strengthen the outlook of the informed (or persuaded) and gradually to catch the attention of others. Campaigns are of course subject to fluctuations in audience attention and to the increasing distraction which eventually develops whatever the interest and quality of the information presented. So the manager's personal skills in communication are most likely to be effective if they are used within the framework of a carefully designed campaign using multi-media and presented intermittently in a maximum variety of appropriate forms.

Check list for the manager

1. How can I ensure that people are adequately informed? In what circumstances do rumours flourish?

    (a) Do staff currently have a great need for the facts? Why?
    (b) If they do, are all the relevant facts readily available? Are they unambiguous?
    (c) If the facts are not available, what steps can I take to ensure that the relevant facts are conveyed clearly to all concerned?

2. Is any of the relevant information distasteful or frightening? If so, what special steps can I take to ensure that this information is still accepted? Can it be presented:

    (a) Gradually?
    (b) Together with help on how to mitigate its effects?

3. What can I do to ensure that my expertise on a relevant subject is known to those whom I have to convince?

4. What can I do to ensure that these people recognise the values we have in common?

5. What power do I have over those I wish to convince. Should I use it? How?

6. When I transmit a message, do I ensure that everyone knows the reason for it?

7. Do I relate all new information to the known interests of those I have to inform?

8. Do I ensure that my subordinates/colleagues work in as stimulating an environment as I can devise for them? Do I present them with relevant/challenging problems, within their capacity to solve?

73

9. When training subordinates, do I ensure that:

    (a) Good work is rewarded and poor work penalised?
    (b) The general framework of their task is made plain from the outset?
    (c) Learning is interspersed with other (interesting/relevant) activities?
    (d) Important lessons are repeated in an interesting variety of forms?
    (e) Difficult or long exercises are grouped appropriately to encourage memory?
    (f) I build on the human proclivity to explore and understand the environment?
    (g) I provide protected situations in which trainees can explore the problem?

10. When giving a talk or writing a report, do I adhere to the structures which relate to what is known about human learning?

11. Do I set my subordinates/myself work targets which are both attainable and challenging?

12. Do I understand, develop, and preserve the conditions in which subordinates/my own attitudes can most readily be reassessed and, if need be, modified?

13. When presenting a case, do I consider the pros and cons of:

    (a) Putting both sides of the case?
    (b) Putting good news before bad?
    (c) Giving major reasons first?
    (d) Stating conclusions?

14. Do I always bear in mind the implications of conveying information to:

    (a) A superior?
    (b) A subordinate?
    (c) A colleague?
    (d) A colleague with rival or competing interests?

15. Do I always bear in mind the implications of all these people conveying information to me?

16. How can I encourage upward communication?

    (a) By providing subordinates with more facilities for communication?
    (b) By using briefing groups?

   (c) By sparing more of my own time?
   (d) By recognising and using the informal leaders?

17. How can I most effectively convey important information? What is the most effective use I and my colleagues can make of all the information media? Do we have an explicit, integrated strategy for conveying information on important issues to all in the organisation?

Further reading

Many of the experiments on perception quoted in this chapter are summarised in:

   Bernard Berelson and Gary A. Steiner, *Human Behavior* (Harcourt Brace, New York, 1964)

Much of the evidence relating to attitudes is summarised in:

   Arthur R. Cohen, *Attitude Change and Social Influence* (Basic Books, New York, 1964)

More recent studies in perception and attitudes are described in McGuire's chapter in the *Handbook of Social Psychology*:

   William J. McGuire, 'The Nature of Attitudes and Attitude Change', *Handbook of Social Psychology*, vol. iii, Ed. G. Lindzey and E. Aronson (Addison-Wesley, Cambridge, Mass., 1969)

The problems of communication in organisations were very well set out in:

   Paul Pigors, *Effective Communication in Industry* (National Association of Manufacturers, New York, 1949)

Several of the field experiments on communication in industry quoted here appear in:

   Business and Industrial Communication, W. C. Redding and G. A. Sanborn Ed. (Harper & Row, New York, 1965)

Questions of self-presentation are discussed in:

   Erving Goffman, *Presentation of the Self in Everyday Life* (Allen Lane, The Penguin Press, 1971)

Skills with people

Some field experiments applying what is known of the learning process to training procedures in industry are described in:

Bernard M. Bass and James A. Vaughan, *Training In Industry: The Management of Learning* (Tavistock Publications, 1966)

Three books dealing with specific points discussed in this chapter are:

R. M. Belbin, *The Discovery Method. An International Experiment in Re-training* (OECD, Paris, 1969)

Derek Rowntree, *Learn how to study* (Macdonald, 1970)

Elizabeth Sidney, *Business Report Writing* (Business Publications, 1965)

A book which critically reviews the contribution of the lecture to training and communication and deals with many aspects of communication in process, is

Donald A. Bligh, *What's the Use of Lectures?* (Penguin, 1972)

4

INTERVIEWING SKILLS

The ability to talk and to listen to another person is central to the effective performance of a manager's job. In this chapter we describe the ways in which the skills of talking and listening are applied to the main kinds of interview which managers tackle.

The selection interview

Most managers have to give interviews to select staff for their own departments, and personnel managers spend a lot of time on this kind of interviewing. A choice of candidates will most probably be made on the basis of information provided in an application form and from an interview. Managers will usually have information from testimonials and preliminary interviews, and sometimes from personality and intelligence tests.

PLANNING THE INTERVIEW PROCEDURE

Before any selection is done it is essential to obtain a job description in order to decide the qualities required. There are several ways of doing this—the detailed activities of which the job consists can be studied by observation and by questioning the job holder and his superior and colleagues. The relative importance of the different aspects and the abilities they demand can be assessed by studying incidents which have led to clear success or failure in the job, or by comparing the attributes of successful and unsuccessful performers. The Job Description must be turned into a Man Specification to provide a yardstick against which to assess candidates. The process is shown below diagramatically. Management Training

Aids developed headings to effect this translation which take account of studies of abilities associated with success in managerial work. These major personality requirements are:

(1) intellectual abilities;
(2) social abilities;
(3) adjustment, maturity, self-understanding and stability;
(4) motivation, drive and direction of interests.

If the technical requirements of a job and any special working conditions (e.g., place of domicile, travelling, etc.) are added, these headings yield a simple but reasonably comprehensive set of categories for matching individuals to the requirements of any managerial job.

Job Description	Man Specification	Candidate
Duties 1 2 3 etc. } requiring { Experience Abilities Special training, etc. } indicating {		Record

The Management Training Aids system requires managers to interpret these terms in a standard way and to collect evidence under each heading from the candidate's record. It also takes into account the need to standardise assessments of information obtained. Variations of the Management Training Aids classification have been adopted by several British companies.

In addition to a Job Specification, the selector needs a well-designed application form and a form for recording and rating the information he obtains. The application form should cover the educational record, work experience, interests, and other information relevant to the job. It should be designed to yield the detailed factual basis about the candidate's record, on which to build a useful interview. In addition to an adequate application form, interviewers need a rating form on which to record their findings. More accurate predictions are made if properly-designed rating scales are used. An example of such a scale is given below:

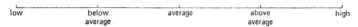

| low | below average | average | above average | high |

Fig. 4.1. Social skills

Five points are as many as an interviewer can use efficiently. He should try to use the scale consistently. For example, he may distribute his judgements on each scale thinking of it as representing a normal distribution curve. This would mean that about 10%, 25%, 30%, 25% and 10% of the total range of possible candidates for the post would fall at different points. This distribution may be an artifact, but it will still serve to help the interviewer apply some consistent standard in assessing the distribution of abilities. The level for the population of candidates also has to be learned by each interviewer. For this he must rely on experience but he can hasten the process by training and by comparing notes with other interviewers.

PLANNING THE INTERVIEW

Before seeing a candidate, the interviewer should prepare himself for the interview by studying the job specification, the application form and other papers about the candidate, and considering the main strengths and possible weaknesses of the candidate. Suitable topics for opening the interview can be noted, and particular lines of enquiry can be planned, to assess the candidate's judgement, stability or whatever may be particularly in doubt. If there are any difficult topics, e.g. medical, these are placed towards the end of the interview.

There are certain conventions about selection interviews. That is to say, there are certain widely held expectations about what happens in this particular social situation. Some commonly held conventions are:

(1) The interview will last between 10–60 minutes; the more important the job the longer the interview.

(2) The interview will consist mainly of the interviewer asking questions, which the candidate should answer. Sometimes these questions may be awkward or personal; this does not matter provided that they are relevant to the job. The interviewer may take notes of the candidate's answers.

(3) The interview is a formal occasion in which both parties are formally dressed, behave politely and are not interrupted.

(4) The interview will take place across a desk or table. This tradition is changing, however, especially with more important and senior jobs, in favour of a coffee table or an orientation of chairs at 90 degrees with no table.

Since these conventions are widely accepted, communication is generally facilitated by adhering to them.

CONDUCTING THE INTERVIEW

Most interviews, including the selection interview, fall into four phases, varying in length and importance according to the interview's purpose. They can conveniently be recognised by the mnemonic, 'WASP':

Welcome. The interviewer greets the candidate and usually begins with some informal chat, seeking common interests or acquaintances, and establishing from the outset the desired relationship. He should also explain the interview procedure briefly, and its part in the total selection process.

Part of the required skill consists of establishing the right relationship—one where the candidate trusts the interviewer sufficiently to feel that he will be properly assessed and is prepared to talk truthfully about his past experience. The interviewer should convey his interest and sympathy with the candidate by appropriate non-verbal signals and should try to understand the candidate. However, he should not take the role of the other to the extent of trying to get the candidate the job. Since there are other candidates to be considered, the interviewer should remain somewhat detached while at the same time being genuinely sympathetic. While the interviewer's role is to carry out selection rather than vocational guidance, he may give some vocational advice if it is asked for. The interview should be a rewarding experience for the candidate and he should feel that he has been properly and fairly assessed.

Acquiring information. This is the major section of the selection interview, in which the candidate's record is carefully explored. One author (Fear) has developed an extensive interview guide indicating the sort of information which may be required. The guide covers four main areas. Abbreviated, they are:

(1) work history, duties, likes, dislikes, achievements, working conditions, level of earnings, reasons for changing job, type of job desired;

(2) education and training, best and poorest subjects, grades, extra-curricular activities, finance of education, training beyond undergraduate level;

(3) early home background, father's occupation, number of brothers and sisters, parental temperaments, discipline, earliest age independent financially;

(4) present social adjustment, interests, hobbies, marital status, health, financial status, attitude towards dependents.

The guide then requires interviewers to rate candidates on certain aspects of personality, e.g., motivation, emotional stability, team work, adaptability, initiative, self-discipline, etc.

The interviewer's non-verbal skills here may consist of a posture and demeanour to indicate a serious, attentive interest in what is being discussed. He may need to deal with shy or nervous people by showing special friendliness and informality, and with the over-confident or brash by rather more formality and briskness. The interviewer should have a definite list of topics to be covered in a certain order: research shows that the interview is more effective when it has a definite plan. These topics often include candidate's family and home background, his education at school and later, his past jobs and present employment, his interests and leisure activities, his attitudes and beliefs, his health and adjustment. The questions can pursue in greater depth what was written on the application form.

It is best not to attach much importance to the candidate's behaviour during the interview; it is a very unusual and rather stressful situation, and most people behave rather differently from the way they behave outside the interview. A fairer picture of how the candidate normally behaves with others is likely to come from questions and answers on how the candidate behaved in various past situations. Similarly, to find out how stable a candidate is, it is better to find out how he reacted to a number of stressful situations in the past than to see how upset he is by the interview itself.

Each aspect of personality can thus be assessed from the answers to suitable questions. For example, attitudes to authority can be assessed by asking questions about past relationships with others of higher or lower status, and attitudes towards traditionally respected groups and institutions, and towards commonly despised social groups. In each area several different questions should be asked, to provide an adequate sample of the candidate's responses. The same aspect of the individual's experience may be discussed in terms which encourage him to reveal his intellectual abilities, his skill with people and his stability or motivation. For example, he may be asked to consider objectively the quality of his education (and so give some indication of his capacity for intellectual analysis), or to talk about the community life of school or work (and so perhaps indicate something of his normal relationships with others). Appropriate questions about examinations, facing new situations, etc., may produce replies which indicate something about his stability. His replies when asked about his special interests and achievements in different circumstances at school may help towards an understanding of his motivation.

A difficulty with this approach is that it assumes that the candidate will tell the truth. No doubt an accomplished liar can do well for himself at an interview, but most people are not accomplished liars and are indeed fairly straightforward. This is not to deny that a candidate will normally try to give as good an account of himself as possible. It does mean, however, that a skilled interviewer who probes for details about past events is likely to obtain a fairly accurate picture.

There are special skills in asking questions. Each topic is usually introduced with an open-ended question, followed by a series of follow-up questions. The interviewer's questions should be responsive to what the candidate says so that there is a proper dialogue or flow of conversation. An open-ended question ('Tell me something about your last job', 'What's your general impression of how things have been going with you over the last year?') is usually difficult to answer in a monosyllable and indeed is an implicit invitation to talk at length. A 'closed' question ('How long were you in this job?') has the reverse effect; it requires a precise, brief answer and is valuable for checking facts. 'Direct' questions should be avoided altogether since they suggest the answer required and introduce bias into the interview. 'Are you efficient?' 'I take it you are a good mixer', etc., indicate which is the right answer. On the other hand, reflective questions and comments ('You enjoyed that part of the work, it seems?' 'You put most of your energies into that side of things?') both encourage the candidate to describe his feelings and attitudes and reassures him that he is being listened to attentively.

Some areas need carefully phrased questions to elicit relevant answers; for example, judgement can be assessed from questions about the candidate's opinions about controversial social issues with which he is acquainted, e.g., student relations with the police, or the situation in Northern Ireland. Special care is needed when enquiring about certain areas, such as physical inabilities, failures, or other potentially embarrassing topics; sometimes the interviewer must discuss these topics in order to match the candidate fairly with the Man Specification. He has to do so, however, in a way which does not damage rapport and prevent the interview continuing usefully. Questions should be asked in a friendly, objective way, and the interviewer should show his sympathy and protect the candidate from loss of face.

A different approach is sometimes used in the assessment of intellectual qualities like creativity and judgement; many interviewers present candidates with problems to deal with instead of asking about past problem-solving. The materials provided by Sidney and Argyle give details of how to assess different traits.

Part of the skill of interviewing consists of being able to deal with awkward candidates. General experience suggests that there are a number of types of awkward candidate that are most commonly encountered, for example the candidate who:

talks too much;
talks too little;
is very nervous;
is bombastic;
plays the wrong role (e.g., seeks vocational guidance, or tries to ask all the questions);
gives an oversmooth presentation;
is unrewarding;
is not interested in the job;
comes from a different class or culture.

Young women can also be difficult to assess accurately, for example, if they turn the interview into a social occasion.

It is clear from this list that an 'awkward' candidate is one who behaves in some way which makes conduct of the interview difficult. He impedes the flow of relevant information and may threaten the interviewer's self-esteem. It is tempting for the interviewer simply to dismiss such a candidate as unsuitable. Some of these behaviours, however, derive from the candidate's lack of experience of interviews and most are compatible with the efficient performance of a wide range of jobs. The interviewer can control many of these and other awkward behaviours by adopting appropriate interview techniques. For example the candidate who talks too little can be dealt with by:

(1) asking easy, open-ended questions;
(2) the use of reinforcement techniques (such as head-nods and 'yes-yes' noises);
(3) the interviewer himself being careful not to talk too much.

The strategy commonly adopted by interviewers is one of looking for weak points in the candidate, i.e. looking for reasons to reject him. This is partly justified by the tendency for candidates to use the complementary strategy, i.e. of covering up their weak points. Nevertheless it would be useful for interviewers to be on the look-out for exceptionally strong points in candidates as well. Again, interviewers are often influenced by their early impressions of candidates based on the application form, clothes, accent, etc. These impressions need to be checked carefully by the collection of further detailed information in relevant areas.

Supplying information. An interview is a dialogue and in all but the most extremely authoritarian situations this carries the assumption that neither side will invariably play the role of either interrogator or respondent. In the selection interview, the applicant can reasonably expect some time in which to ask questions himself. Preferably he should not have to ask general questions about the organisation (these are most accurately and economically answered in booklets, etc.) nor even general questions about the job (which can be supplied in a written job description). But he may still have specific questions about the relation of his own circumstances to the demands of the job and the working environment and, in any event, he must have the opportunity to ask questions. He may want to know conditions of service, to challenge sources of evidence, to understand the reasons behind decisions, etc.

It is arguable whether these questions should be answered before or after exploring the candidate's record. If the answer to a question will determine whether or not the candidate remains interested in the post, it should be dealt with early ('Now, before you start telling me about yourself is there anything about the job which we should discuss right away?'). In general, however, it is best to get the candidate talking first about his experiences. Taking an active part in the interview helps to reduce any anxiety he has. The interviewer also obtains information which helps him to understand the significance of any questions the candidate asks subsequently.

Parting. The close of a useful interview tends to show an increase in the non-verbal behaviours which state the relationship between the parties. However, before these concluding and more personal remarks, the close of the interview is likely to be heralded by a summary, from the interviewer, of any agreements reached and, most importantly, of any plans for practical action. This has the effect of reducing anxiety or other emotions which the interview may have aroused and also of confirming that the interview has been worthwhile. Thus an interviewer, according to the purpose of the meeting, might conclude with a remark such as: 'We have two more people to see this week and we shall be discussing the appointment on Friday. So you will hear from me, either way, by Wednesday next week at latest. Please let me know, meanwhile, if you should decide to withdraw your application.'

Even if the candidate is rejected it is still important to send him away satisfied that he has had fair and courteous treatment.

An interviewer who pays attention to this aspect of his task is establishing a good relationship for his firm with a wide public. He can reasonably hope thereby that recruits of good calibre will not be deterred from presenting themselves as future candidates. He can certainly assume that if he establishes a poor relationship, that candidate will go away disturbed and may neither join the company nor encourage his friends to do so.

EFFECTIVENESS OF THE INTERVIEW

How effective is interviewing as a means of selection? It is most relevant to compare the accuracy of selection made on the basis of academic record, testimonials, test scores, etc., with and without an interview. A number of studies show quite clearly that the addition of the interview raises the validity of selection from about ·3– ·4 to ·5– ·6. Secondly, it is found that some interviewers are very much better than others, so that clearly interviewing would be more effective if only the 'right' people did it. The correlation between an interviewer's ratings and measures of the later success of candidates have been found to vary between ·15–·65. It is also found that interviewing is more successful for some personality qualities than others. Interviewing is most accurate for social skills and motivation, least accurate for mental abilities. Effective interviewers are characteristically similar to their candidates in age and social background, are intelligent and well adjusted, are introverted rather than extroverted and have been trained to use the most effective interviewing skills.

One organisation studied the effect of different interviewers on candidates' decisions as to whether or not to continue with their application to join. The percentage of candidates who accept invitations to come to a second interview were found to vary from 30 per cent to 80 per cent for different interviewers, even when the standards for referral appeared constant.

When assessing and rating the information he has obtained,

the interviewer may fall into a number of common errors as follows:

> *errors of 'level'*, a tendency to rate all candidates on average too high or too low;
>
> *errors of 'spread'*, using too large or too small a scatter of ratings;
>
> *stereotyped judgements*, based on the social class, race, sex, long hair, etc., of candidates;
>
> *search for consistency*, failure to recognise that a candidate may be clever but lazy, etc.;
>
> *implicit personality theory*, having private theories, implicit or explicit, about which traits should correlate together;
>
> *'halo' effect*, putting undue weight on limited information so that it is used as the basis for judgement on all aspects of behaviour. A special 'halo' derives from the limitations of role relations in the interview. The interviewer assesses the candidate as the person he saw at interview. It is difficult to imagine a candidate's behaviour outside the interview situation—yet his behaviour at the interview may be quite atypical.

A manager needs to guard against these biases in himself. In this respect it is helpful if he can discuss his conclusions with other interviewers in a selectors' conference. Before such a discussion, his own conclusions must be drawn from consideration of the evidence, gathered at the interview, about the different abilities and qualities the candidate has shown. The resulting rating should then be matched against the Man Specification.

There is also a problem about *reliability,* i.e. the extent to which interviewers agree with each other about how a set of candidates should be rated. The interview is somewhat less reliable than other methods of assessment, partly because the same candidate may react differently to different interviewers and partly because different topics may lead to his being seen in a more or less favourable light. Here again it is helpful if the candidate is seen by two or three interviewers who meet after the interviews, pool their findings and try to reconcile their ratings from the often complementary material obtained

In a board interview, three or more interviewers may see the candidate together. Board interviews have the drawback that it is not possible to establish such a good relationship as in an individual interview. Boards make some candidates very nervous whilst a few benefit unduly from their skills of self-presentation. In addition, the interviewers have only one encounter with the candidate on which to assess him.

Apart from validity and reliability of interviewing there is also the question of its utility, i.e. what is gained against the time and expense involved. The costs of selecting highly-skilled or educated people, such as graduates, have now become so high that this has become an important consideration. Some firms compromise and weed out the less serious applicants by asking candidates to fill in a lengthy questionnaire. Indeed a very elaborate biographical questionnaire has been used with some success as a cheaper alternative to an interview proper.

The appraisal interview

Many organisations have recently shifted from emphasis on recruitment and selection—bringing in the most appropriate talents—to appraisal—developing and correctly using the talents already employed. Thus the appraisal interview is playing an increasingly important part in many modern managerial systems. It is a regular (usually annual) review of a subordinate's performance, and future works plans and personal prospects, usually conducted by the subordinate's immediate superior. Properly carried out, the appraisal interview is helpful in assessing and developing individual abilities; and as a link between individual needs and motivation, the organisation's provision of training, promotion, salary progression, etc., and the organisation's plans for managerial succession. It is also an important additional (sometimes corrective) form of communication between manager and subordinate.

A modern appraisal system standardises (1) ways of assessing current performance and (2) ways of assessing individual potential. It requires both parties to begin by agreeing work objectives. Goals to be achieved are decided as precisely as possible, a date set for their completion and a standard set by which the level of achievement shall be judged. The appraisal interview then becomes a review of progress held at intervals dictated by the target dates. The individual's contribution is set in context. Some part will be attributable to the fortunes of the department or even to the organisation as a whole. Some part will be attributable to the way he has been supervised. Some will be fairly attributed to the individual's own strengths or weaknesses.

As evidence on the individual's contribution accumulates, a constructive discussion can develop to consider ways of improving his current performance or of developing him for further responsibilities. This type of procedure is most thoroughly developed in target setting, a technique often related to management by objectives, first defined by Peter Drucker in the 1950s and applied to appraisal by Douglas McGregor in 1957. Its growing appeal to UK managers may be because of the relationship it presumes to prevail between managers and subordinates. Business schools and departments of management studies usually promulgate the values of democratic leadership, and many younger managers see the advantages of a relationship of *primus inter pares* where they control others by means of a democratic discussion and in the light of established facts.

An objection to target setting is that it is very difficult to define objectives and standards of attainment for many jobs. However, it seems that these difficulties are often exaggerated. Research is an example of work sometimes thought to be inimicable to target setting where targets have in fact been successfully applied. Equally the Electricity Council found target setting could be applied successfully to a wide range of more junior staff as well as to senior and professional managers. Many other firms have reached similar conclusions.

One review of failures of target setting appraisal suggests that most serious problems derive from failure to accept the implied philosophy or else failure to recognise that philosophy's limitations. Thus target setting failed when appraisers believed that it was sufficient to agree targets and 'let the facts speak for themselves'. 'Democracy' and 'objectivity' do not absolve the manager from the need to assess individual strengths and weaknesses once the results have been discussed. It also failed with managers who did not fully accept the implications of mutually agreeing targets. These managers tended to set targets for subordinates and then coax them into acceptance.

A manager must also guard against the danger that target setting might not tackle the issue of preparing an individual for further responsibilities. This is an important aspect of any adequate appraisal system. One study showed, in fact, that target setting could have the effect of limiting appraisal to short-term objectives and underrating the man who was building for the future. An adequate appraisal system should include provision for a discussion of the subordinate's future aspiration and his long-term training needs.

APPRAISAL INTERVIEW OBJECTIVE

One company has spelt out the objectives of the Appraisal Interview as follows:

(1) review past targets and objectives as a basis for setting better future targets;

(2) review performance of the subordinate in achieving or not achieving his targets, in order to help him improve his performance in the future;

(3) review future career aspirations and planning so that both company and individual needs are met;

(4) clarify misunderstandings and rectify attitudes and

assumptions which may be hindering an effective working relationship;

(5) produce records for appraisal system and for forecasting manpower needs;

(6) grade and assess subordinate's performance and tell him where he stands in his boss's estimation.

Despite these potential advantages, appraisal systems do not always work well and many managers avoid conducting appraisal interviews.

Many reasons are put forward for this avoidance. The great majority indicate a distaste or embarrassment over the interview because of its presumed effect upon normal work relationships. It may appear to the manager to require a formal judgemental relationship which he is ordinarily careful to avoid, or it may seem to demand a detailed close understanding of the subordinate's job which the manager sees no ordinary need to possess. Then the appraisal interview, as opposed to completion of an appraisal form, does demand some participation and mutual discussion of the subordinate's performance and the goals he should set himself.

One survey showed that some managers find it difficult to welcome or encourage a participatory role in their subordinates. Another experiment on the effects of high and low participation showed that whilst high participation on the part of the subordinate had generally beneficial results, a certain number of subordinates themselves had difficulty in participating. These subordinates were used to very little participation in their normal dealings with their superiors, and they felt more at ease when this normal situation prevailed in the interview, and work targets were simply assigned to them.

Some appraisal systems have indeed implied a relationship which a modern manager would find very difficult to sustain in everyday work with responsible subordinates. These systems required a manager to rate a subordinate on a series of personal qualities with little guarantee that these qualities were important in effective work performance. In the subsequent interview he was expected to inform the subordinate how he had been rated. However, in the last few years many companies have moved towards appraisal in terms of job performance (e.g., agreed definition of assignments and objectives; evaluation of quality and performance; definition of areas of excellence and areas requiring improvement). The effect has been to bring appraisal very much more into line with normal day-to-day relationships between manager and subordinate and so to reduce substantially the problems posed by the appraisal interview.

PLANNING THE INTERVIEW

An effective appraisal interview (whether to set initial targets or to review on-going progress) demands considerable preparation. Increasingly, both manager and subordinate are involved in this—both have to review the subordinate's recent progress and both may have forms to fill in. Appraisers should be clear about the reason for the appraisal and what it is to achieve. They should be careful to appraise on the basis of sufficient, relevant and representative information, and should assess the evidence honestly. To ensure adequacy of information, a manager needs to keep interim notes of a subordinates' performance and may need to refer to personnel records (e.g., to check on absences, illness, etc.). Assessments should be reached tentatively and proffered at the interview as (carefully considered) opinions, open to discussion.

CONDUCTING THE INTERVIEW

Welcome. Following the 'WASP' plan, the manager needs to pay particular attention to settling the subordinate down, since most subordinates feel apprehensive about this interview.

Acquiring Information/Supplying Information. The interview itself is likely to begin with establishment of the facts. Manager and subordinate agree the subordinate's job description, consider whether his duties have changed and agree the targets set and achievement attained since the last review. From this stage of agreement on the facts, a discussion can develop as to why targets were or were not attained. Neither success nor failure can be accepted at face value since targets may or may not be attained for a variety of reasons each with different implications for both parties. Some targets are not attained for reasons genuinely outside the subordinate's control, possibly for reasons which implicate the manager himself and his running of the department. Eventually manager and subordinate must come to review the subordinate's contribution to the results and must make an assessment of his demonstrated strengths and weaknesses. Subsequent targets are then agreed together with practical steps to improve the subordinate's performance where necessary, and (taking into account his aspirations and hopes) to prepare him for further responsibilities.

The objectives and plan of this interview requires of the manager a sophisticated set of interviewing skills. It assumes a dialogue with the interviewee taking an active part in the discussion. The two aspects of 'acquiring information' and 'giving information' kept separate in other types of interview, must be mixed and blended into suitable proportions according to the subjects under discussion. This is a joint discussion; the manager is using the participation style of management described in Chapter 7. There is some evidence that subordinates will welcome this style of interview even when it is not typical of the manager's general style. In the study above the majority of subordinates did benefit from participation, which was found to make for: more goals being achieved; better understanding between appraiser and subordinate; improved attitudes towards appraisal and more self-realisation on the job.

At different points of an appraisal interview a manager will find himself using a variety of social skills which are described more fully elsewhere in this book—persuasion, problem-solving, counselling and listening.

94

To encourage a positive, constructive attitude towards any problems which the interview establishes, the manager can use questions directed towards problem-solving, rather than judgement, for example:

Feelings about the job

How do you feel about your job?

Are your duties and responsibilities clear to you?

What part of your job do you consider most important?

What suggestions do you have for improving our department?

Do you find your job sufficiently challenging?

Do you have any queries about company plans for this department?

Performance of the work

What part of your job do you find easiest and most enjoyable?

What part of your job do you feel you do particularly well?

Where do you feel there is greatest room for improvement in your work?

How can I help you do a better job?

Other subjects

What are your long range goals?

What are your plans for reaching these goals?

How can I help you?

How do you feel about interviews like this?

These and similar questions will encourage the subordinate to produce his evidence and views. For his part, the manager, having done his homework as we suggested earlier in this chapter, must be prepared at the appropriate moment to state his objectives and views, and those of the company, as persuasively as possible. This will involve a frank discussion of strengths and weaknesses.

A difficulty may arise if the subordinate's poor performance is really attributable to poor leadership; here the manager must be honest but he is also required to represent the organisation and his own position fairly. Thus he cannot pass blame on to others, even when this would seem entirely justifiable, and when acknowledging his own fallibility he must also try to put it in some sort of perspective for the subordinate.

Then there is the question of giving praise or blame. In a study of praise and blame it was found that praise was usually vague and general and had little effect. Subordinates dismissed it as insincere and waited for the phrase which indicated that criticism could be received objectively. The more criticism was given, the more defensive the subordinate became, and the less improvement did his performance show in subsequent weeks. The subordinate's defensiveness in the face of criticism is understandable enough. Managers dealing with unsatisfactory subordinates should deliberately decide to try to gain agreement for improvement on one or two important issues. Thus a little progress might be made each time, where telling the subordinate all his faults might not result in any. Praise should be as specific as possible—immediate and rewarding feedback is a strong stimulus to improvement.

Finally, the plan does tend to assume that both parties are committed and interested to develop the subordinate as fully as possible in accordance with the needs of the organisation. This assumption is not always justified. The manager's desire to develop his subordinates may shrivel when he sees an able junior increasingly challenging his own position; or when promotion of a junior entails the slow and painful process of finding and developing his successor; or when all the effort the manager has devoted to developing others' talents appears to be ignored by his own superiors. Many managers do find satisfaction in developing subordinates—but not to the point of self-immolation. Chapter 6, dealing with individuals, discusses some of the ways in which a manager may need to protect himself in these circumstances, if his organisation will not do so, while still retaining a constructive role.

Subordinates, too, are not always willing and anxious to improve. They may be prevented by limited ability, or by a general defensiveness which cannot admit to any weakness. Highly able people may be unwilling to master the skills of a humdrum job. Some subordinates do not feel for their superiors the minimal trust and respect which any constructive dialogue presumes. These and similar situations call for the use of non-directive and counselling skills. The manager may thereby gain a better understanding of his subordinate's personality, attitudes and motivation. The subordinate may be helped to understand himself and his needs in relation to the work and the company, and to take more responsibility for his own decisions and work plan.

Parting. The interview must conclude with a summary of topics covered, agreements reached and future action to be taken by both parties. The manager should restate his intention to be a support and resource to his subordinate and encourage him to discuss any problems with him in the interval before their next meeting.

Personnel interviews—counselling, problem-solving, grievance

Selection and appraisal interviews are much more likely to be successful if the interviewer is clear about his purpose and uses the interviewing skills appropriate to his purpose and his plan. This objective and systematic approach is also helpful in conducting interviews with apparently vaguer objectives. These will include personnel interviews conducted to counsel someone in difficulty, to help him reach a decision or to resolve a grievance.

DECIDING THE PURPOSE AND PLAN

Wherever possible, the manager should find time to consider in advance the purpose of the interview. This kind of preparation is not possible when the interview develops spontaneously from a crisis situation (e.g., a subordinate in personal distress), but here at least the immediate objective is likely to be clear. Reasons for the counselling interview may include all or some of the following:

to help the interviewee let off steam;
to help him to see himself or his problems more clearly;
to support him while he finds his own solutions and makes his own decisions;
to demonstrate interest and genuine concern.

An essential skill in achieving these purposes is listening. Listening has been described as the lost art of our age. Managers in particular are required to spend much time exhorting, persuading, explaining, arguing, discussing intricate technical problems—all the forms of communication required to run complicated fast-moving technical systems. They are much less often required to listen with great concentration. Hence questions are asked but the reply is not heard. Judgements are based on inadequate evidence and facts accepted at their face value. In the sense required for these interviews listening is a forceful dynamic activity. To 'hear' the true meaning of what a person is attempting to tell—a meaning perhaps imperfectly understood by the speaker himself and one in which attitudes and feelings may be inextricably mixed with facts—the interviewer needs to concentrate on what is being said to the complete exclusion of any other thing. His approach must be 'permissive' but searching—until he is assured that he truly understands the other person's viewpoint.

The effective listener is by definition himself silent for much of the interview. He should try not to take up more than 25 per cent of the speaking time. His plan should be to listen for the latent as well as the manifest content of remarks. Each sentence will reveal something about the speaker's background, experience, attitudes and values.

Such statements as 'They were a poor crowd there', or 'It was an unhappy ship from the moment we sailed', carry the manifest meaning that these particular groups seemed to the speaker inadequate or ill-matched. Similar remarks repeated through an interview, however, may reasonably be interpreted by an interviewer as 'I am a bad mixer, I cannot get on well with other people and so all groups I meet seem unattractive to me'. An intent listener 'hears' words which primarily convey emotion and so recognises the presence and strength of an attitude which underlies the words.

A graduate with a wealthy father applied for a post in a chemical firm. His interviewer needed to discover whether the young man was serious about a career. The young man explained that he had won an industrial scholarship and stated 'so I did well financially and had no need of the State'. The interviewer replied, 'Or, indeed your father?'. The young man answered, 'No, certainly not my father'. The emotion in the word 'certainly' began to illuminate this young man's fierce spirit of independence.

Silences, hesitations, what is *not* said also yield valuable evidence to the perceptive listener. A silence of omission, a short answer, a hesitation before a remark, may indicate a reluctance or inability to share some experience with the interviewer. Or there may be a struggle to sort out thoughts in order to express them clearly. A perceptive interviewer will recognise this process and remain silent himself—as one author has said, 'Every interviewer should have the four-letter word "WAIT" stamped indelibly on his consciousness'.

Finally, the interviewer can obtain useful information about an interviewee from the language he uses. Much of the language we use expresses feelings as well as objective facts—tone of voice, choice of words and phrases and sentence construction—are all highly personal. Probably no interviewer is quite insensitive to this double function of language but many are powerfully affected by it without appreciating the source of their reactions. The skilful listener distinguishes carefully

99

between sentences which describe only facts and remarks which, though spoken as facts, are describing opinions, feelings and attitudes as well. He recognises language as a source of information about the personality, attitudes and opinions of the person who is using it and tries consciously to interpret the messages it carries.

CONDUCTING THE INTERVIEW

Welcome. Following the same 'WASP' pattern the welcome, non-verbal and verbal should aim to establish a sympathetic non-threatening atmosphere. Enquiries about some aspect of the interviewee's personal life may sometimes be appropriate: stating the purpose of the interview nearly always is.

Acquiring information. It is particularly important in these interviews to establish quickly an accepting atmosphere of 'timeless calm' in which the interviewee can feel secure enough to express his real thoughts and feelings. This is done by the use of encouraging non-verbal signals, by the adoption of a permissive, objective, patient attitude, and by appropriate questioning technique. A middle-aged woman interviewed this way observed, 'We were mostly me working together on my problem as I saw it'. The interviewer had placed his own attitudes and needs on one side, and had so entered into her personality, understanding how she felt and thought that he had become her 'other self'. C. G. Jung has described the attitude which this approach demands. 'We get in touch with another, with an attitude of unprejudiced objectivity—a kind of deep respect for facts and events and for the person who suffers from them.' P. E. Vernon speaks of the need for an interviewer to be 'unshockable', able to accept any statement as true for the interviewee however odd or unpalatable it might appear to the interviewer. Hence the interviewer suppresses his own personality. He does not argue or evaluate, but tries to ask questions or rephrase statements so that the respondent begins to see his own problem more clearly.

A manager demonstrated that he understood a statement made by one of his girl clerks, 'that she would rather work in a publishing firm because the latter was more artistic and the people were different and much more interesting—like my last boss who dictated lying on the floor' when he replied, 'In fact you feel you thrive more on an unconventional atmosphere?'

The interviewer cannot remain a passive listener. At times the subject will almost certainly need help in expressing himself and the interviewer must be ready with questions. These can be categorised in three ways: questions to elicit facts; questions to elicit consciously held attitudes, and questions which aim at an exploration of deeper attitudes (possibly not consciously formulated by the interviewee himself).

All interviews call for the establishment of some basic facts, but the counselling and problem-solving interviewer, having asked for a minimum of facts, should proceed to ask for feelings, either consciously held or more deeply rooted, using the same open-ended type of question already described. Here is one example:

> *Interviewer to interviewee* (who had worked as a journalist and was currently very uneasy about his job prospects): 'Why did you change to the Daily X?'
>
> *Interviewee*: 'The openings were not so great on the Daily Y.'
>
> *Interviewer*: 'Do you find greater satisfaction working for the Daily X?'
>
> *Interviewee*:—pause—'I've never thought about that, I don't think one even thinks about this.'

The second of these questions probed a feeling which the interviewee had not adequately explored within himself, and thus helped him to see his own motivation more clearly. Or, a shorter example:

> *Interviewer:* 'What type of work do you do now?'
>
> *Interviewee:* 'I supervise.'

Interviewer: 'Do you like being in charge?'
Interviewee: 'Do I like being in charge? . . . that's a leading
question' . . . pause . . . 'No, I don't.'

A summarising or 'reflecting' remark can demonstrate that the
interviewer understands 'with' the interviewee. For example,
when a bus driver observed, 'When the passengers come round
to the front of the bus and say "Thank you", you feel you've
been appreciated like', and the interviewer reflected, 'This you
feel is part of the satisfaction of the job.' 'Yes', replied the bus
driver—'Yes, I do.'

A person needing help in solving a problem and coming to a
decision, needs a large proportion of analytical probing
questions. The interviewer will find himself asking such
questions as:

Would you tell me more about that?
What did you do then?
If you did that what would A's reaction be? Who else would
be affected?
How do you think you should handle that situation?
Why do you say that?
What are the advantages, and disadvantages, of such a
course?

An interviewee who is feeling very frustrated or emotionally
disturbed may find probing of this kind less useful. He may
be best helped by the use of a high proportion of reflecting
remarks, which reassure him about the interviewer's understanding, and allow him to speak freely about his negative
feelings and reduce the emotional pressure.

The interviewer conducting this type of interview will
evoke negative reactions of fear, hostility or suspicious
withdrawal if he does any of the following:

Fails to stay neutral or criticises ('Surely that's an odd
attitude to adopt?')
Misunderstands.

Jumps to conclusions (*Interviewee*: 'I like figures and procedures better than people.' *Interviewer*: 'You find it difficult to deal with people?' *Interviewee*: 'No!')

Deals with the situation arbitrarily ('I think that solves your problem.')

Rejects interviewee ('I don't think there is much point in continuing this discussion.')

When a person with a problem has been helped to talk about it he will often see the solution for himself. W. E. Beveridge cites several case histories with this result. For instance, one man discovered that the solution to his problem was to leave his present firm. A shorthand typist who began by stating that she wished to hand in her notice ended by asking if she could withdraw it. A social worker employed by a voluntary agency was helped by her interviewer better to understand her relationships to her committee and to decide what concrete proposals to make to them to enable her to do an effective job.

A manager is often tempted to influence the other by giving him advice: there is a welfare officer in most of us struggling to get out. Most of this good advice is ignored, however, if only because it is usually inadequately adapted to the individual's needs and personality. Analytical listening helps a person to produce his own solutions and reach his own decisions. These are very much more likely to be translated into action, because they are appropriate to his needs.

Supplying information. The range of information which may be asked for in the counselling interview is much less predictable than it is for the selection or appraisal interview. The counselling technique itself may promote responses which amount to important new information for both interviewer and interviewee. Some problems simply require straightforward factual information to put them in perspective. ('You can start drawing your pension at fifty-five'). In addition to supplying information, the interviewer can offer to supply further help. Whilst improved decisions are seldom translated into action, help in carrying out a decision the interviewee has made himself is likely to be accepted.

A successful counselling interview, which has manifestly helped the interviewee, is exhilarating for both parties and the interviewer may have to be careful not to commit himself or the organisation to action beyond his authority to carry out. Since the manager is not only a sympathetic counsellor but also a representative of the company and of higher management, he will probably need to change at the appropriate moment from listening to persuading or informing. He may need to say 'I've heard and understand your point of view, now listen to mine.' He may need to reiterate company policy, restate departmental objectives or standards, or call attention to the interviewee's poor past record (e.g., poor performance, absenteeism, late coming, etc.).

Relevant facts need stating as precisely as possible, e.g., the chances of promotion from a particular post, company policy on a particular issue, likely completion dates for work in hand, and so forth. However, whilst he must still give accurate information, it is also reasonable for him to make sure that any relevant attractive information is supplied. For example, if promotion chances are slim, it may be relevant and fair to the organisation and to the candidate to tell him this, but also to mention the work's variety or training potential. If delivery dates are far ahead, it may be relevant to mention to a colleague or buyer any standards of quality, guarantees or servicing which could offset this disadvantage.

Because of his representational role, the manager is usually also required to give information objectively, without discussing individuals or personalities. There are occasions when this is a temptation which takes some resisting. The manager may strongly suspect, for example, that a dispute has developed simply because the issue has been clumsily handled by a particular person. But there are many good reasons why in most interviews it may be unwise to say so. For one thing, a scrupulous concern with the facts, rather than with blame, is one way of reassuring the interviewee that anything he himself says will be objectively considered. Then it is often more disturbing than reassuring to hear that others working in one's own organisation are to blame. No doubt one source of this unease is the threat to self-respect that is implied if one has invested effort in so fallible a situation. Not only, the interviewee may feel, does his organisation harbour people who handle situations badly, but it also apparently tolerates superiors who look for scapegoats when faced with trouble.

Parting. A summary and plans for future action are as important at the end of this type of interview as in selection. Thus the interview, according to the purpose, might conclude with remarks such as these:

'We'll meet again on Tuesday, when we have both had a chance to talk to Personnel and decide which training course would best suit you.'

'I do now see why this dispute/problem has arisen. I will see what can be done about making the company's requirements more explicit and we will both talk to (X, Y, Z, etc.) and meet again next week.'

Check list for the manager

1. What is the purpose of the interview? What can I hope to achieve? What does the other person hope to achieve?

2. What information do I need before starting the interview? Is it obtainable? If so, when can I study it? If not, how will its lack affect the interview?

3. What is the best plan for the interview?

4. What relationship should I establish? How do I establish it?

5. What information should I collect? What information should I convey? How do I convey unwelcome news?

6. What type of question should I ask, to encourage the other person to talk; to keep him to relevant issues; to check on the facts; to help him describe his feelings?

105

7. What can I do or say to make him feel assured of sympathy? To encourage mutual understanding?

8. How do I conclude the interview? How do I ensure that the interview does not damage any on-going relationship? What can I do or say to ensure a practical and constructive outcome?

9. How can I encourage decisions leading to practical action, with allocated responsibilities for performance?

10. After the interview, should I record the decisions? Who should be informed about them? What form should the record take?

11. What is my plan for carrying out my responsibilities? For helping the interviewee to carry out his?

12. What plans should I make for follow-up?

Further reading

The skills and techniques involved in selection interviewing are described in:

Elizabeth Sidney and Michael Argyle, *Course Manual: Selection Interviewing Training Programme* (distributed by Management Training Aids (Mantra) Ltd., 1969)

R. A. Fear, *The Evaluation Interview* (McGraw-Hill, New York, 1958)

Biases in selection interviewing are reviewed in:

E. C. Webster, *Decision Making in the Employment Interview* (McGill University Industrial Relations Centre, West Montreal, 1964)

Biases in personal perception, such as arise in the interview, are reviewed in:

R. Tagiuri, 'Person Perception', *Handbook of Social Psychology*, vol. iii, Ed. G. Lindzey and E. Aronson (Addison-Wesley, Cambridge, Mass., 1969)

The contribution of the selection interview to effective selection is reviewed in:

L. Ulrich and D. Trumbo, 'The Selection Interview Since 1949', *Psychological Bulletin* **63**, 110–16, 1965

A classic study of practices in appraisal interviewing is:

Kay H. Rowe, 'An Appraisal of Appraisers', *Journal of Management Studies* vol. i, no. 1, Mar. 1964

A more recent review of company practices in appraisal is supplied in:

'Human Quality Control', The British Institute of Management Information Note No. 66 (Apr. 1967)

Much practical advice on the conduct of appraisal systems and interviews is supplied in:

Marion S. Kellogg, *What to do About Performance Appraisal* (American Management Association, 1965)

The classic work on counselling technique is:

Carl Rogers, *Client Centred Therapy* (Constable, 1965)

Techniques for personnel interviews are reviewed in:

William E. Beveridge, *Problem Solving Interviews* (Allen & Unwin, 1969)

A general review of interviewing is contained in:

Elizabeth Sidney and Margaret Brown, *The Skills of Interviewing* (Tavistock Publications, 1961)

A general review of the difficulties and effectiveness of selection procedures is contained in:

M. D. Dunnette, *Personnel Selection and Placement* (Tavistock Publications, 1967)

5
USING MEETINGS AND COMMITTEES EFFECTIVELY

Purposes of meeting or committee

Most managers find themselves, at some time or another, attending meetings or serving on a committee. A few serve on so many that this activity seems to account for much of their time. In industry and commerce meetings serve many different purposes and have different amounts of power to make or influence decisions.

BRIEFING ON PROGRESS MEETINGS

This is held by a superior with subordinates to keep them informed or to outline plans and procedures he wishes them to implement. Such meetings have no decision-making powers but usually include an exchange of views and may result in a list of action points, with specific people held accountable for their completion by specified dates.

CONSULTATIVE MEETINGS

Other meetings are called by a manager to collect the views of his subordinates or to ask for solutions to problems. The manager consults, but retains the right to make the final choice. Brown and Jaques call these 'command meetings'. Another type is a discussion held between colleagues to solve a problem or to establish a common outlook, a 'collatoral meeting'.

COMMITTEES

None of the foregoing are decision-making bodies and they are properly called meetings rather than committees. A

108

committee is, specifically, an instrument for solving problems and reaching decisions. Thus, for example, a coordinating committee, intended to keep different departments working on the same lines, is a misnomer unless decisions can be taken which are binding upon the departments concerned. A safety committee is just that if it is empowered to decide on such matters as implementation of safety regulations, but not if it is a group discussion run by the departmental manager, who has no intention of allowing the group to decide anything about which he himself is not entirely happy. The members of a committee are there (or should be there) only because each one can help in reaching a good decision. They may not be there as individuals; indeed, more probably they are there to represent others—trade union members, shop-floor workers, a specialist department, a professional group. The decisions taken by a committee must be accepted by all members as the committee's view and put forward and supported as such by them. Minority groups who disagree with the majority strongly enough may be able to get their views recorded, but in the end they must accept the majority opinion or resign. This holds for the chairman, as well as for everyone else.

A large group of middle managers was asked by one company about their estimate of the usefulness and efficiency of the committees they attended. Their views ranged from 'very useful . . .' to 'absolute waste of time'. Exactly the same range of opinions appeared in a survey covering 1,200 subscribers to the *Harvard Business Review*. The first step towards setting up a meeting or committee, therefore, is to define its purposes, its powers, its responsibilities, and to get general agreement on its terms of reference. General agreement on these issues does not prevent a committee, for example, operating on occasion as a briefing or consultative meeting. The chairman may introduce one item on the agenda with, 'I want to keep you in the picture' (briefing), the next with, 'Can we have a decision on this, please' (committee decision), and a third with, 'Let's hear all views on this' (consultative). The requirement is simply for general agreement about what the meeting is empowered to do and clear directions when this role is temporarily changed. Informal *ad hoc* committees and meetings require this type of direction as much as large and formal gatherings. They can equally be rendered ineffective and their members disillusioned if they lack this essential guidance. This not only turns committees into a more effective instrument but enables members to see their usefulness, the more important since investigations show that many managers feel committees and meetings are a waste of time.

Skills of managing meetings and committees

Defining the committee's purpose is the first step to effectiveness, but many more skills are required if the committee is to run smoothly and productively. Some of these are concerned with the organisation of, and planning for, the work of the committee, some are interpersonal skills which both chairman and committee members need to learn.

THE ORGANISATION OF THE COMMITTEE

Studies of behaviour in groups consistently show a number of patterns of interaction which can be anticipated and taken into account when planning a meeting. Members of any group have strong needs for interaction with each other and there appear to be fairly narrow limits, in terms of numbers, within which these needs are most likely to be met and combined with effective intellectual achievement. Pairs, threes and fours are frequently more concerned with establishing and maintaining satisfactory personal relationship than with intellectual progress. On the other hand, groups which are too large for individuals to establish some personal relationship with all the others, show an increasing tendency to fragment. They are likely to show the increasing dominance of a general hierarchy and increasing frustration on the part of members who have little opportunity to take part in proceedings. These frustrated people soon begin to break up into small cliques and sub-groups concerned to preserve their own interests rather than contribute objectively to the committee's tasks. Order has increasingly to be preserved, not because all the members accept the necessary personal discipline, but by the exercise of rules of procedure.

As a general guide, committees and meetings probably ought to consist of not fewer than five or more than fifteen people. Within this range other relevant factors are frequency, number of meetings and the nature of the committee's task. People who meet frequently and often or even regularly, over a long period, have the opportunity to establish relationships and may be able to develop into a stable, unified group even when numbers are large. Some tasks, such as drafting or fact finding, are always best performed by small groups.

Once the committee has been appointed the manager responsible can do much to help it function efficiently. An obvious step is to arrange meetings sufficiently regularly and frequently for the committee to get on with establishing its own relationships and gain practice in accomplishing the task. It is probably sensible for new committees to meet fairly often just for this reason. Subsequently, they may need to meet less often. Regular meetings, however, are undoubtedly always helpful, since they can be planned for and the risk of individual absence reduced. A manager can take many conscious steps to weld his committee into a team in the early days of its existence. Pride in belonging to the committee can be deliberately fostered. For example, people work well with others whom they are glad to work with. Cooperation in experimental group work has been influenced by telling individuals beforehand that their group is considered exceptionally well/ill suited in terms of personality, exceptionally distinguished/ limited in intellectual ability and so forth. People work hard too in groups which they believe are doing a worthwhile job, which have clear objectives, which they believe have standing and prestige and whose members are approximately equal to themselves in status, expertise or ability. They are least interested in working for groups without authority and with great discrepancies in ability and status between the members.

All these conditions apply to committees, and explicit statements about them should be made and adhered to. The chairman should take positive steps to ensure that each committee member believes his task to be worthwhile. Initially this may involve seeing individuals separately to discover what their attitudes are and to persuade them, if necessary, about the importance of the work. It may also entail personal discussions with individual members, outside committee work, to ascertain their current feelings and assure them of the value of their presence. This procedure can do much to reduce frustration and increase efficiency as long as it is applied to all the committee members and not apparently reserved for a chosen few. The real powers of any committee should be made known and the special qualifications of its members made clear. Some committees may be important enough for all this to be published or put up on a notice-board. All are important enough for their chairman to define their powers, and welcome members in a way which recognises their potential as contributors. In addition, chairmen need to take especial pains to establish the potential equality of contribution of any junior or apparently low-status people on his committee. Equally, whilst a committee's decisions are issued to outsiders as a group view, this does not prevent the chairman crediting individuals with special achievements and effort within committee sessions.

PLANNING AHEAD

Before the meeting the chairman should make a flexible plan of campaign to suit the particular purpose of the committee. He must acquaint himself with the range of subjects and points of view likely to be expressed. He needs to prepare his opening statement particularly carefully. In it, he should define the meeting's purpose and responsibilities, introduce the agenda and propose a timetable; all with neutral objectivity. Thereafter he should keep to time and as a minimum ensure that all available facts are stated and weighted before alternative solutions are suggested and decisions reached.

Committee members can be told in advance what they are expected to do and can be given some training in the skills of discussion. Experiments suggest that people benefit, for example, from being told explicitly how to cooperate. One famous experiment required a group of people to pull conical corks out of the same bottle; each person had his own wedges to rescue. The groups appeared unable to cooperate even though cooperation effectively solved their individual problems, until briefed to cooperate rather than compete. An extensive field study of seventy-two committees in different organisations showed that committees felt greater satisfaction if run to a pattern, with rules of procedure and the assurance that everyone would have a fair hearing. Some of this control is provided by normal committee procedure. A chairman is expected to ensure that his committee is supplied (usually by the committee secretary) with the papers it needs, in ample time. Committee members who receive an agenda, minutes of the previous meeting and background papers are also being informed *ipso facto* that the meeting has a serious purpose for which they need to prepare.

Where these procedures seem inadequate and a committee continues to prove unruly, an imaginative chairman may be able to introduce more discipline by taking special measures. One chairman of a voluntary committee found that normal committee procedure did not prevent committee meetings regularly running seriously over time. Committee members frequently wandered from the subject and raised issues not on the agenda. Rather than fall into a continuously repressive role during meetings, the chairman introduced other procedures:

H

113

Skills with people

(1) He established pre-committee meetings with the relevant officials, at which all background papers and issues likely to be raised, were discussed.

(2) He established the procedure of asking the author of each background paper first to speak on it. He then asked the other officials for comments thus ensuring that the facts were known before starting a discussion.

These measures helped gradually to bring the meetings under control.

Skills of committee members

Being a productive committee member involves many qualities —expertise or representational abilities relating to the subject matter, ability to talk relevantly and effectively; an ability to subordinate personal ends to the objectives of the meeting and of those one represents. The field study quoted above produced a high correlation between frequency of use of the pronoun 'we' and the group's satisfaction with its progress. Groups became dissatisfied when they contained a high proportion of apparently self-centred individuals who spoke to gain points and attract attention or used the group as an audience for their views. By contrast, humble contributing people help a committee, because they invite (and receive) help; the cooperative are rewarded by others' cooperation. A detailed analysis made by Bales of the contributions of different members showed that groups have standard characteristics in the way they deal with problems and use the time available. Many early remarks in a discussion are to define the task and the group members' function. The number of helpful constructive contributions gradually rises. Somewhere in the middle of the discussion members begin to discourage any new ideas, and subsequently demand general acceptance of the solution. This involves increasingly strong controls and more negative discouraging remarks. At the conclusion,

114

however, there is a rapid increase in positive remarks, as though the group fear the destruction of the pattern of interaction it has achieved. A member's popularity depends (obviously) a good deal upon his contributions. Expertise, production of ideas, and warm and rewarding remarks all increase the individual's popularity. Members also value different characteristics at different times. In the early stages, those who contribute most are valued, presumably if only because they provide a starting point for interaction. Later, those who speak a good deal but not most of all, become more popular. At this stage the group has presumably become aware of the limitations of its noisiest members. Contributions are still essential but not when they limit the contributions of others.

Thus being a good committee member involves both interacting helpfully with others and helping the group achieve its task. A good committee member needs to be:

(1) knowledgeable on the committee's subject;

(2) interested in helping the committee to make progress;

(3) conscientious in preparing for committee meetings, studying documents, collecting information; concerned to save committee's time (e.g., by careful preparation, by preventing interruptions during committee, by arriving on time);

(4) prepared to put his point of view clearly and vigorously;

(5) able to keep to the point;

(6) able to listen to other points of view, interested in others' ideas, capable of being convinced by them;

(7) Disciplined and patient, not demanding excessive time for his own point of view, ready to recognise the authority of the chair;

(8) reliable in carrying out the committee's decisions as they affect him.

He will show his skill in:

(1) producing new ideas;

(2) helping to clarify and develop other ideas;

(3) recognising and expressing interest in others' views;

(4) listening;

(5) helping to keep discussion to the point;

(6) asking for clarification and for summaries of progress as necessary.

Skills of chairmanship

Nevertheless, the way the chairman fulfils his role is the key factor. He has to help the group to make intellectual progress, but he also has prime responsibility for maintaining a team spirit, with each individual feeling recognised and concerned to give of his best. This dual task requires sophisticated skills and many generally competent chairmen are not equally good at both aspects. Sometimes the tasks are divided. Thus one highly efficient logical chairman works regularly with a friendly vice-chairman with a pleasant welcoming manner. Conversely a comforting rewarding chairman often receives more or less unobtrusive guidance from committee members who can think logically.

DEALING WITH THE 'HIDDEN AGENDA'

Many chairman find it difficult to realise that their committee is operating on two levels simultaneously. While apparently working on the intellectual task their discussion and intellectual effectiveness will be continuously affected by the 'hidden emotional agenda' present in all social interaction. This 'agenda' is 'hidden' because it has apparently no connection with the surface task and does not appear on the formal agenda. By and large it is composed of all the feelings, ambitions, beliefs, attitudes and special needs of individual members (or the people they represent) which cannot be openly expressed lest they threaten the group or the individual's position in the group. One member may have brought along his own 'hip pocket' solution and will be waiting for an opportunity to slip it in. He may have an axe to grind or he may be more competent than the others. Others may come as delegates rather than as representatives. They become uneasy if decisions seem to threaten their 'back home' group. There will be, too, inevitable clashes of personality; bids for power and hostility towards leadership. Some members may not like the task. Others will become easily bored.

The chairman must learn to recognise the types of hidden agenda present in his own meetings and make correct judgements about when to suppress them and when to encourage their open expression. If feelings become too strongly negative the hidden agenda can take possession of the meeting and wreck decision-making. At one committee meeting about the production of a document, the chairman (a woman) had been annoying members by her autocratic behaviour. One member particularly resented this and, as his temper rose, the following exchanges took place. The member said, 'One small point, the letter "I" should not be used in paragraph seven because it might be confused with the figure "one".' The chairman replied, 'I don't think that is very important.' This remark further irritated the member and a little later he rose to his feet and said, 'I would ask madam chairman's indulgence if she's got any. She hasn't shown much today.' He then made his point and another member called out, 'I can't hear.' Madam chairman replied, 'I'm sorry, Mr. X. is not speaking very clearly.' In this exchange, the chairman and committee member are dealing with the hidden agenda rather than the papers before them. This type of personal conflict can be very difficult to handle. A more percipient chairman, however, would have recognised the challenge in X.'s first remark and perhaps called for others' views to deal with it. She would also have protected X. later, by simply asking him to make his point again more loudly. When the subject for discussion is known to rouse strong feelings, a chairman may often

117

forestall trouble by acknowledging this and asking for their open expression, 'Now I think there will be conflicting views on this issue, can we hear what people really feel about it?' "Reflecting" remarks can also be used to make explicit the hidden agenda. Thus, in a discussion about the value of committee meetings, one member said, 'I find meetings are often a waste of time, discussing things which I have nothing to do with.' 'Yes,' said another, 'I often find myself taking forty winks.' The chairman "reflected", 'You feel meetings are sometimes boring.'

RECOGNISING INDIVIDUALS

The chairman gives particular recognition to individuals at the outset of the committee's work, or when any special contribution warrants this. But he also continuously acknowledges the value of each person, e.g., by smiling or by using encouraging remarks such as, 'Yes, I see your meaning', 'Interesting', or 'Thank you'. He acknowledges specific contributions in such statements as, 'Mr. X., you are adding a point to what Mr. Y. said some while ago.' A question is useful in place of criticism or argument and for discouraging the talkative and encouraging the shy. If trouble looms he can back track to look for more facts, or show where agreement has been reached. Against this the chairman needs to control those powerful personalities who might irritate or even destroy the group. A variety of skills may be needed to control dominant and destructive members. Some practical examples could be observed in the work of the chairman of the voluntary committee, quoted earlier. For example this chairman had to deal with Dr. R., a member who advised on research and development matters. This committee member was a very creative person who had solved many difficult problems. But he was also difficult, speaking at great length, and pouring such scorn on the ideas of others that he threatened the committee's continuing function. The chairman and other committee members learned to retain his contribution and protect the group by the following methods.

(1) The chairman and some of the members would discuss (usually individually and by 'phone) each meeting beforehand. They would agree the issues on which Dr. R. *must* be consulted and would also agree implicitly that he would *never* be actively consulted on any other matter.

(2) On occasion, the chairman would rearrange the agenda to ensure that 'Dr. R. items' came up towards the end of the meeting.

(3) In committee, the chairman (and to some extent the members) developed considerable skill in appearing to invite comments from everyone whilst actually passing over Dr. R. If Dr. R. did contribute on the 'wrong' subjects, his comments were simply received politely. Some less experienced members gradually learned without explicit guidance not to promote discussion with him.

Another example. Miss G. represented an important department in a regular meeting of senior colleagues in an organisation. The organisation was changing and growing extremely fast. It was a situation which involved considerable strain for the senior staff, most of whom, however, found a reward in tackling the unexpected, creating precedents and even dealing with crises. The exception was Miss G. She had a good analytical mind and could argue well against any proposed development. She could also quote precedent and authorities to show that any new proposal would never work. In a situation which seemed to many to be full of potential excitement, Miss G.'s persistently predictable reactions provoked great irritation. The chairman and certain committee members developed various means of handling this situation.

(1) The chairman often asked her to comment first on any new proposal, because he was sure of her disapproval and

119

sure that this would stimulate support for the idea from everyone else.

(2) One committee member relied on cajoling: 'Well, Susan, now you've told us why it won't work in your usual brilliant style . . .'

(3) One member worked hard to collect even more evidence and precedents than Miss G. could produce in order to refute her argument.

By these means Miss G.'s real contribution of analytical caution was retained, but her disruptive influence was neutralised.

The chairman must also be scrupulous to recognise minority views. This behaviour is essential if he is to fulfil his function as well as possible. In one experiment, a rewarding and welcoming chairman asked persistently for minority views. His style of chairmanship irritated the more talkative but resulted in the solution of more problems.

ASKING QUESTIONS AND SUMMARISING

An important technique of chairmanship is the use of questions. Instead of himself making statements beginning with 'I think . . .', or 'Yes, but don't you see . . .', or 'I don't agree with you', the skilled chairman uses phrases such as 'What do you think about . . .?', 'What do we know . . . ?', 'What do you mean . . . ?', 'What is the significance of . . . ?', 'How much importance should be attached to . . . ?', 'Do you feel strongly . . . ?', 'Can we turn to this other aspect . . . ?', 'Can we take point A first?', 'Mr. X., can we hear your views?', 'Can we turn to this other aspect . . . ?'. Sometimes these questions will be directed to the whole group, sometimes to a particular individual. A submissive group may ask the chairman to supply much of the information, ideas and decisions himself. The chairman can avoid accepting this role by redirecting the request. Searching questions from the chair can uncover information, facts and opinions, call attention to problems or ideas, or to another phase of the subject. Questions can clarify the strength of feeling or support for an opinion or a disagreement, and can direct thinking back to first causes.

Another important technique is summarising. 'We have agreed to do 1.', 'The points of view which have emerged are . . .', 'Our solution to 2. seems to be . . .', 'We are still disagreed about 3.', etc. Summaries enable the group to confirm or modify their decisions, and to assess what progress is being made. Summaries also help the chairman to keep control without appearing dictatorial and enable the secretary to record decisions accurately. A final summary prevents much subsequent misunderstanding. The chairman must avoid summarising too early or summarising with a bias which too strongly reflects his own view or the view of one section.

SUPPLYING A SENSE OF PROGRESS

The chairman must supply drive and purpose, so that committee members feel that progress is being made. Remarks such as, 'So we've settled point A, now we can turn to point B', or a summary prefaced by a remark labelling progress made and followed by, 'We now have two or three further decisions to make', serve to identify areas covered or still to be covered.

CONCLUDING

The chairman's closing remarks are as important as his opening statement. He should conclude with a summary of progress made and action required. If problems remain unresolved, he should state the next step. He must be scrupulous both to record true progress accurately, showing a positive confidence in the committee's work, and also to state fairly the issues still to be dealt with. Remaining disagreements cannot be glossed over without risking a sense of futility. In all, the chairman is custodian of the group. He fosters it, keeps it together, protects it from disintegration and futility and helps it achieve its task. This demanding job is seldom compatible with taking an active part in the discussion. The chairman who does this may become involved and lose control of the meeting. At the very least he may confuse his committee members, who are no longer sure who is in charge or if he speaks as one of them or as a voice of higher authority. Chairmen should therefore, in general, not contribute to discussion and if they do, should make clear their changed role—'If I may leave the chair for a moment I would like to say that . . .'.

Various expedients have been tried in situations where the chairman found difficulty in remaining in role. The same person might be required as an active committee member and, because of seniority, as chairman. A particular manager might simply be unable to master a chairman's skills.

One solution has been to put a junior person in the chair, leaving the senior free to contribute as an ordinary committee member. Where there is not too much discrepancy in status, and where relationships are fairly informal anyway, this may work effectively. An independent chairman of similar status to the senior member may be appointed from outside the organisation simply to run the meeting. In the United Kingdom a lay chairman is sometimes appointed to run a Government scientific committee or investigating body. It is conceivable that large companies might benefit if they were to second suitable managers, simply to move round chairing their important committees. It may be possible to rely on very clearly defined terms of reference and on the sophistication of the chairman and committee members in sorting out these different roles.

A case study

Description of case and discussion	*Comments and interpretations*

(1) A Managing Director held regular meetings at his headquarters office with the works managers of his four manufacturing units.

The agenda normally included some items for discussion or advice, some for briefing and some for joint decision-making. The Managing Director was skilled at chairing.

(1) Regular meetings kept the lines of communication open. The importance of all the items to them and the skill of the Managing Director, made these managers feel the committee meetings were worthwhile.

(2) An item for joint decision-making, the training of supervisors at the factories, appeared on one agenda.

(2) A suitable subject to deal with in this way.

(3) The Managing Director opened the discussion with the words, 'I think our supervisors need training, I propose to call in training consultant firm Y. to do this. I should like your decision as to whether we train them here at H.Q. one evening a week or for a whole week consecutively.' (He then outlines the specific training subjects; mainly on the handling of people, the skills of persuading and skills of negotiating with shop stewards and of dealing with complaints, and discipline matters.)

(3) Not a neutral enough briefing. It alarmed, or annoyed, two out of the four works managers. One had elderly supervisors whom, he knew, would resent training; the other felt this was a veiled criticism of his supervisors. The third felt the Managing Director was an autocrat and he could think of many other ways of implementing training schemes. The fourth works manager was young, newly appointed and eager, therefore, to support the Managing Director, whatever he proposed. This 'hidden agenda' of personal and factory interests profoundly affects the subsequent

123

Description of case and discussion	*Comments and interpretations*
	discussion. Prior planning and thought by the Managing Director would have alerted him to some of this.
(4) *Manager A.* 'Well, supervisory training is a good idea, but shouldn't we managers go through it first? We should know what our subordinates are being taught.'	(4) Manager A. does not want to sound negative but proposes something which will help him with his back-home difficulties.
(5) *Manager B.* 'I think you are right—what's more supervisors could do a better job if we *all* knew more about the overall picture. H.Q. is often secretive and remote.'	(5) Manager B. springs to the defence of his supervisors in a roundabout way.
(6) *Managing Director.* 'These are two good points—you feel we *all* need training?'	(6) Managing Director 'hears' the hidden agenda and makes an encouraging and 'reflecting' remark. He shows he accepts his works managers by doing this and helps them to express their true opinions.
(7) A discussion ensues on these points. More examples are given and Manager A. eventually mentions the age of his supervisors.	(7) This discussion reassures Manager A. to the extent that he can mention his real difficulty.
(8) *Manager C.* 'Why don't we hold a training-cum-information session for works managers and supervisors at a hotel in the country? It could last five days and we could discuss future company policies and plans as well as holding specific training sessions.'	(8) A testing statement . . . How autocratic *is* the Managing Director?

124

Description of case and discussion	*Comments and interpretations*
(9) *Managing Director.* 'Can we look at the advantages and disadvantages of this proposal?'	(9) Managing Director shows he is willing to listen, but asks analytical and clarifying questions. This makes his managers think and justify their arguments.
(10) Manager D. then supports the original proposal of the Managing Director.	(10) The first statement of this manager's 'hidden agenda'.
(11) A long discussion follows. Managers A., B. and C. develop their theme, the Managing Director asks questions, summarises points made but does not argue.	(11) The Managing Director is pursuing his prime objective. He wants supervisory training —but does not care too much about its form.
(12) Managing Director then summarises. 'So what we might do is for all of us, plus the supervisory staff from the four production units, to go to a country hotel for five days. Training sessions would be interspersed with talks and discussions about the company's future plans and objectives.' To Manager D., 'Would you agree to that?'	(12) This new proposal is better than the Managing Director's original one and takes care of the 'hidden agenda'. The Managing Director is careful to gain commitment from Manager D. (who is quite happy to agree as his main objective is to appear cooperative).
(13) The committee then goes on to discuss practical plans and administrative details concluding with a minute on the action to be taken by each manager.	(13) The Managing Director is satisfied with these results. He feels he has used his committee constructively and gained his own main objective.

Why use committee meetings?

A large number of experiments have been conducted relating to this question. Conclusions from this evidence are that, although individuals produce more ideas, groups perform

125

better in criticising ideas and putting complicated ideas together. The inventive members may be stimulated by hearing each other, and the people with critical judgement help to eliminate the poor and impractical notions. Groups also do somewhat better than comparable individuals working on their own in analysing complex problems. Comparisons of groups of slightly different size (groups of four versus groups of six to eight) suggest that smaller groups reach workable decisions more rapidly, whilst the larger groups produce more ideas and better analysis of problems. Five is the number people prefer: three to six works well. Larger groups also do better than smaller on analysing complex matters, presumably because they have more intellectual resources to draw upon. However, these results all appear in relatively small groups. It is not, unfortunately, true that increasing a group's size above these figures will result in a comparable improvement in intellectual performance. On the contrary, a diminishing return in terms of productivity begins to appear—one study has suggested this occurs once the group gets into double figures. These large groups are increasingly dominated by a few personalities while potentially valuable contributors remain silent.

Committees are also a vehicle for different kinds of expertise to be tapped. Some years ago an inspection problem in a small company was resolved partly by introducing a committee procedure. The company was making precision equipment and instruments, many of them incorporating special modifications requested by scientific customers. The difficulty of reducing waste and raising standards of inspection of these products to an acceptable level was proving intractable. In the end the problem was solved by considerably increasing the training and expertise of the relevant operatives, and also by introducing regular small meetings between operatives, superiors and inspectors. This gave formal recognition that all could contribute to the maintenance of high standards.

The average judgement of a group also seems to be better

than the judgement of comparable individuals working alone. A group's average estimate of simple measures, such as height, tends to be better than the best individual estimate. Its judgement of more complex matters, including assessment of ambiguous and non-quantifiable material, tends to be better than the individual judgement of most of its members, apparently because the group is persuaded by the arguments and confidence of the most knowledgeable people present. The proviso is that, as in the example just quoted, if a group is to achieve good judgements the members must represent a variety of opinions. If all the people present share substantially the same ideas, the result of the meeting will simply be to strengthen them in their views, whether or not these are correct. Interaction between members with different outlooks corrects errors and stimulates ideas. The presence of others stimulates greater commitment and members formulate their suggestions more carefully than if they were alone. Given that these different conditions are present, groups apparently do have an advantage over individuals in dealing with certain sorts of intellectual problems. They are likely to produce more and better ideas and solutions, may reach a better understanding and interpretation of complex or ambiguous material and a sounder judgement on both practical and ambiguous issues.

Another powerful reason for using a committee is that a decision taken by a group is more likely to be carried through by its members. They feel committed, not only because they have helped in making the decision but also through their relationship to the rest of the group. This topic is discussed further in Chapter 7.

WHEN NOT TO USE COMMITTEES

Management by committee, however, if used inappropriately can be a cumbersome and inefficient decision-making instrument. Committees are worse than individuals at working out courses of action, relating information together in some logical sequence or dealing with simple organisational matters. Some experiments too, have shown that groups make riskier decisions than individuals. An individual tends to make riskier decisions as he thinks a problem over, and will also commit himself in a group to something riskier than he would chance on his own. Though not proved, this might be because he feels his responsibility is shared, and also because the group is likely to be dominated by its most extroverted and ambitious members. Of course, the risk involved in a decision is separate from its quality. Some risks may be very well justified, and others not, but it is a factor to be considered before asking a committee to decide on an issue.

Managers should pay particular attention to these negative findings, since people's feelings about the committees on which they serve are affected by them. Members can see the advantages of discussion for tackling some problems, but will suffer frustration and irritation when the agenda is filled with inappropriate items. So many managers have suffered in this way that committees have become very unpopular with a vast majority. The skilful manager will therefore, take care to prune such items from his agendas or even be prepared to disband committees saddled with tasks which could be accomplished more effectively by other means.

CONCLUSIONS

The lesson for committees in industry and commerce is this: committees should be formed from experts able to contribute to the intellectual problems who, between them, will represent a number of divergent viewpoints, knowledge, skills or expertise. Given this variety of outlook, committee membership should be limited and the group helped to form a strong, friendly relationship as rapidly as possible. Both it and its individual members should be protected from unreasonable threats. A committee will be the most appropriate tool to use for complicated decisions requiring highly specialised knowledge or the balanced judgement of many variables. Committees too are capable of the creative and lateral thinking needed in modern industry and commerce. In addition, the sorts of problem best tackled by committees are likely to develop at certain phases in a company's history. Major reorganisations, teething troubles over the development or marketing of a new product, changeover to new systems, may all require many people to interpret new and confusing information, without the benefit of past experience, and to make important decisions on limited evidence. In these circumstances, there are great advantages in setting up a committee composed of a cross-section of the people involved.

TRAINING PEOPLE IN COMMITTEE WORK

The skills required to work effectively in a committee can be taught. Several methods of training have been outlined by Dr. Anstey in a book entitled *Committees, How They Work and How to Work Them.* Training for committee work is also described in Chapter 9.

Appendix: Further experimental evidence

Experimental evidence on the relationship of patterns of communication between individuals and their ability to deal with problems collaborates our conclusions about the uses of committees. Harold Leavitt arranged for groups of five people to work in circles, chains, Ys and wheels in Fig. 5.1.

The arrows indicate direction of communication permitted to each person. His work showed that simple tasks requiring organisation of material were most efficiently solved by people working in wheel and Y patterns. Those in the circle eliminated errors quickly but could not organise an agreed solution. In the wheel and Y shapes, people at the centre of the pattern enjoyed themselves, whilst others did not. In the circle, everybody enjoyed themselves. The depressing implications of this

I

Skills with people

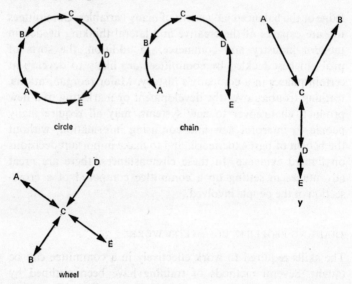

Fig. 5.1.

are offset by the results of work with more complex problems. In trying to reach agreement on interpretation of ambiguous information, circle people came to more accurate conclusions more rapidly than people in the other patterns. Most industrial groups are organised in more or less complicated versions of chains, Ys or wheels. But a committee, because of its collective responsibility is, inevitably, a more or less complicated version of a circle, unless it has a very firm chairman.

Experiments have shown that people in groups influence each other and behave in various non-rational ways. Chairmen should note these when considering types of hidden emotional agendas present in their committees.

(1) Strongly established groups act as one in alarming conditions (they may be collectively braver or collectively more alarmist than less integrated groups).

(2) Other experiments have indicated the strength of pressure

130

which groups can exert upon deviants. Groups deliberately briefed to make obviously erroneous judgements about the length of a straight line were able to persuade one-third of a number of innocent participants that the group judgement must be right, against the evidence of their senses. These rather disturbing effects particularly tend to appear when people are overawed by high-status people making better judgements than others or when the atmosphere is authoritarian, suggestible or frightening.

(3) The advantage of a well-established friendly group is its resilience in frustrating circumstances; the members may grow aggressive but they all continue to attempt to tackle the problem.

(4) Other experiments, of which the most famous must be the experiment undertaken during World War II to persuade American housewives to serve their families offal meats, indicate that members of groups influence each other to change their habits if they discuss the matter and commit themselves individually to some new course of action.

Action points for a manager chairing a committee

1. Decide if a committee is the best instrument for handling the present situation.

2. Determine if its objectives, terms of reference and authority to make decisions or recommendations are clearly defined and up to date.

3. Decide if the membership is appropriate to the task and the right number.

4. Ensure each member understands the committee's objectives and continues to feel committed to achieving them.

5. Ensure each member has been trained in committee skills.

6. Give detailed attention to the achievement of clear and efficient administrative arrangements for the committee.

7. Learn the skills of conducting a meeting and of preparing a plan for the committee in advance.

131

8. Devise procedures for translating decisions or recommendations into action.

9. Check at regular intervals the continued usefulness of the committee.

Further reading

General books dealing either wholly or in part with the skills involved in committee work:

Edgar Anstey, *Committees: How they work and how to work them* (Allen & Unwin, 1965)

Michael Argyle, *Social Interaction* (Penguin, 1969)

R. F. Bates, *Interaction Process Analysis* (Addison-Wesley, Cambridge, Mass., 1950)

Some of the more important research studies referred to in this chapter are described in:

Harold Gnetzkow (Ed.), *Groups, Leadership and Men* (Carnegie Press, New York, 1951)

J. W. Thibant and H. H. Kelly, 'Group problem solving', *Handbook of Social Psychology*, vol. iv, ed. G. Lindzey and E. Aronson, Addison Lesley, 1969

Harold J. Leavitt, 'Some Effects of Certain Communication Patterns on Group Performance', *J. Abnorm. Soc. Psychology*, vol. 46, 38–50, 1951

S. E. Asch, *Effects of Group Pressures upon the Modification and Distortion of Judgements*, H. Gnetzkow (Ed.) (Groups, Leadership & Men. Pittsburgh Rutgers University Press, 1951)

Lester Coch and J. R. P. French, 'Overcoming Resistance to Change', *Human Relations*, vol. i, 512–32, 1947–8

6

THE MANAGER DEALING WITH INDIVIDUALS: LONG-TERM RELATIONSHIPS

DEALING WITH INDIVIDUALS TAKES MUCH MANAGEMENT TIME

There must be few managers who have not complained that it would be easy to get on with the job if only someone would stop the interruptions. Rosemary Stewart found that more than half of the day of the average middle manager is taken up with quite brief contacts, queries, confirmations, progress chasing and the like. Leonard Sayles observed managers in an automobile plant. They spent an average of 44 per cent of their day in brief discussions with subordinates, colleagues and superiors, meeting some hundreds of people. In an electrical equipment manufacturing plant, managers observed spent an average of 52 per cent of their day on such discussions. These encounters were not long planned interviews or meetings. The shortest recorded discussion lasted three-quarters of a minute and the longest five minutes. For these managers, formal interviews, meetings, correspondence, visits and so forth had all to be fitted in to what remained of the working hours.

These events are not 'unnecessary' or 'interruptions', but the warp and woof of management. It is not a question of well-thought-out, dynamic administrative processes being broken up by trivia; but that a manager has been appointed precisely to conduct meticulously (and to a constant standard) this continuing stream of detailed, often personally frustrating encounters. Some of them will make considerable demands on his patience, persistence and equability; many will demand social skill and others will demand quick thinking and good judgement. Each one which is handled successfully contributes to the manager's standing and effectiveness and builds him a credit against the next encounter. Each one bungled has the reverse effect.

The range of roles required of the manager

Almost by definition a manager is in charge of subordinates. He is also certain to be involved in a number of encounters with colleagues. He has to deal with managers from whom his department receives materials or information and with others to whom he in turn transmits his department's products. He has to deal with managers supplying the services essential for his department to work effectively, and similarly with outsiders supplying services, materials or advice. For many managers, the trade union representatives are prominent in this list. Finally, every manager will certainly be accountable to someone. Some managers (e.g. those in service departments) may have several bosses. The most senior people in an organisation, usually the directors, may be accountable apparently to rather nebulous groups such as shareholders and government departments, and for implementing national policy and so forth. Despite the variety in these relationships, it is possible to see persistent requirements between all managers and all bosses.

SKILLS AND ORGANISATION OF STRUCTURES FOR
SATISFACTORY RELATIONSHIPS

The skills of handling people which are required for these situations need to be supported by appropriately organised structures. A structure in which roles, responsibilities and patterns of communication are ill or wrongly defined can defeat the most intelligent interpersonal behaviour, just as much as clumsy treatment of others can offset the advantages of an appropriate structure. It is therefore important to look at both these elements in effective interpersonal skills. Considerable and consistent evidence points to the following requirements for building satisfactory relationships:

(1) Roles and responsibilities need defining and upholding.

(2) All levels require information about work, standards of performance and working circumstances.

(3) All managers have to represent their departments to others and to the outside world.

(4) Everyone needs some job satisfaction and some commitment to their work.

In this chapter we consider the first three requirements. In each case we look first at the way of organising the structure and then at the social skills involved, as seen from three points of view; that of the superior, the colleague and the subordinate. In Chapters 7 and 9 point (4) is covered.

Though some relationships require different treatment there is also some considerable overlap; structures and social skills effective for fostering good relations with subordinates often prove equally effective when applied to relationships with colleagues or superiors. This is depicted in the following table.

Being a superior	*Being a colleague*	*Being a subordinate*
(1) *Definition and upholding of roles and responsibilities*		
Organising a structure		
Define roles and lines of authority and conditions of service.	Define relationships between roles.	Ask for role and relationship definitions.
Social skills		
Keep up-to-date; train and explain.	Learn and use trading, bargaining and negotiating techniques.	Ask for, and maintain, communication channels with superior.

135

Being a superior	Being a colleague	Being a subordinate

(2) *Information on work and standards of performance and working circumstances*

Organising a structure

Provide induction procedures and written job descriptions. Provide an appraisal system.	Systematic communication procedures.	Same as for colleagues.

Social skills

Train and explain.	Communicate honestly the facts of the case. Maintain acceptable standards of work.	Same as for colleagues.

(3) *Representation—relationships with other departments and the outside world*

Organising a structure

Protect roles by defining status positions.	As for superior.	As for superior.

Social skills

Learn skills of persuading and negotiating. Learn skills of self-representation.	As for superior.	As for superior.

(4) *Developing individual job satisfaction and commitment*

Organising a structure

Enrich jobs. Build work groups.	Spread the idea of job enrichment. Encourage team spirit.	Inform superior if job is unrewarding, or team spirit lacking.

136

Being a superior	Being a colleague	Being a subordinate
Social skills		
Provide a supportive atmosphere.	Generate sense of fairness and enthusiasm.	Show appreciation of superiors support and good work.
Give general supervision.	Communicate.	Communicate.
Delegate.	Take personal interest in individuals.	Take personal interest in individuals.
Take personal interest in individuals.		
Use democratic and persuasive leadership style.		

Definition of roles and responsibilities

BEING A SUPERIOR

A definition of roles begins with designing a structure. The first process, selection, requires all those concerned to describe each job to be filled, to define its limits of discretion, and to ensure as far as possible that each person appointed is working at tasks appropriate for his abilities and ambitions. Each subordinate should know who is his immediate boss. The latter's span of control should be small enough to enable him to understand, motivate and lead his subordinates. The subordinates' pay and conditions of service should be commensurate with the skill and level of responsibility of his job and should be integrated into a company personnel policy which relates these conditions fairly to the rewards given to others within and without the organisation.

This structure is a support, but the manager must still ensure that definition of each role required of his subordinates, and the rewards it earns, are kept up to date. He must ensure that role and rewards are clearly understood and (as need be) adjusted to a subordinate's abilities. This is done by being

137

present in the work situation, by on-the-job training and by regular interviewing. One woman welfare officer inherited her job from a man. It took her boss several months to learn that she found two parts of it particularly distasteful—inspecting the men's toilets and inspecting a warehouse infested with rats! The job description had not been reviewed at her appointment and her superior had neither given her training nor discovered her views.

BEING A COLLEAGUE

Good job definitions can do much to aid colleagues to co-operate smoothly. In particular, the interrelationship of roles needs careful definition, especially those between line management and specialist functions. Accountability for results needs to carry with it the right to specify what is to be done, where and at what cost. Functional management carries the right to prescribe how the operation should be carried out. The status of service departments requires skilful handling. Line managers often resent the freedom of access which service managers seem to enjoy both to superiors and to subordinates. They resent the expert who knows the answers but does not accept responsibility either for carrying the solutions through or for their ultimate success. They resent the amount of policy information which is fed into head office service departments, and the way in which head office invests systems of control which are 'unworkable' in the field. Uncertainty about status needs to be programmed out in advance. As an example, it should be known who is to prevail in a conflict between a line manager and a member of a staff department (possibly junior but an emissary from a powerful headquarter's department), or which of two competing departments is to receive priority in the allocation of services. A common superior may have to be recognised as the final arbitrator (Fig. 6.1).

Even given an appropriately defined relationship, however,

138

many situations must always depend heavily upon the skill with which the individual manager establishes personal contacts. Where relationships are good, much information, vital to effective performance, is transmitted in casual conversation. Other background information is relatively easy to obtain. A sense of 'fairness' is more easily developed if only because the work load is more enjoyable, people are less concerned to keep detailed accounts as to who does what and whether everyone is contributing equally. In general, work proceeds more smoothly if colleagues maintain a sustaining, cooperative, friendly role, if they convey a conviction of the other's competence and goodwill and, above all, if they are

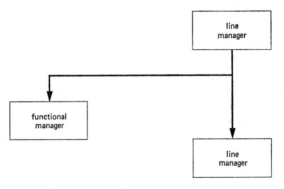

Fig. 6.1.

ready to minimise possible status differences and show a willingness to put questions of individual responsibility in perspective, in terms of the total good.

But within this general framework, how are colleagues trying to influence each other? Sayles finds a trading, bargaining, negotiating element common to many peer situations. Every manager is likely at different times to become a 'buyer' trying to acquire scarce resources or expertise, or a 'seller' trying to heighten demand for his department's products and services.

139

Often he is negotiating, offering to modify terms and conditions in return for improved services.

The 'buying', 'selling' and 'negotiating' process is strongly affected when one party has clearly more authority or status than the other. But when relative status is ill-defined other criteria for responding to individuals grow more important. Friends, people who are personally rewarding to deal with and those who are powerful, tend to have preference. Preference may also be given to the person who shares some important value, e.g., a manager may prefer either colleagues who always meet their target dates, those who produce a first-rate service or those who may be able to return help in the future. He may also simply prefer a colleague with whom he shares quite extraneous interest, perhaps religious, political or sporting.

Sayles further notes that successful 'buyers' and 'sellers' use standard selling techniques. As a 'seller' the skilful manager makes sure that colleagues are aware of the value of his product; this is a continuous apparently casual process, not necessarily related to a particular deal. 'Buyers' acquire scarce resources by pointing out the advantage to suppliers of dealing with them rather than anyone else. A particular problem arises with service departments. Since it is uneconomic to staff service departments to meet occasional peak demands, there are occasions when services are in short supply. At these times, 'customers' try to ensure their own supplies by frequent appeals and exhortations. The effect may be that precisely at a time of crisis a service manager spends more time answering calls than getting on with urgent work. Successful service managers develop ways of reducing these effects. They introduce schedules and publicise their services to encourage their use outside times of crisis. They give careful explanations, if the service is under pressure, and they ask for cooperation. A 'customer' who can offer space, or manpower, or who can alter the time he needs the service, may then be accommodated even at very busy times.

NEGOTIATING AND BARGAINING SKILLS

Successful negotiation depends a good deal upon a judicious mixture of formality, with appeals to logic, and informal reliance upon the appeal of friendship, future cooperation and so forth. In one experiment subjects were given objectives for which to bargain. One person was given a highly extravagant objective, the other a 'reasonable' one. Subjects worked in pairs, but their methods of communicating were controlled. Sometimes they spoke face to face, sometimes by telephone; sometimes they were allowed free conversation, sometimes required to state their case in turn, without interruption.

Results showed that the person with a 'reasonable' objective did significantly better when speaking on the telephone and when each side stated the case without interruption. The experimenters conclude that those whose cause is 'just' should aim at formal discussions, where reason may prevail. Those whose cause is weak or extravagant should prefer informal situations where they may be able to influence by virtue of their personality.

Some understanding of the other's point of view is necessary before a satisfactory solution can be developed. Morley and Stephenson quote an experiment in which negotiating teams decided in advance either to hold unanimously to an opinion, or to present a range of views including that of an extremist. The 'best' solution emerged when two teams negotiated, each offering a range of views—apparently because this increased the areas for discussion and possible agreement. In another experiment, some negotiators argued their own case whilst others were required to change over and argue their opponent's case. The most imaginative solutions were reached when negotiators argued their opponent's case. The subjects, however, reported feeling very uneasy and dissatisfied with the experiment. Perhaps agreeing too much with the other person's point of view constitutes an excessive challenge to personal integrity?

141

EVIDENCE FROM TRADE UNION–MANAGEMENT
NEGOTIATIONS

A summary of several studies of trade union negotiations
suggests that effective negotiations follow a fairly standard
pattern:

(1) Initially both parties state their position as forcefully
as possible. This is a formal stage when the speakers are
recognised as representing their organisation. One study showed
that any attempt to mitigate differences at this stage weakened
the effectiveness of subsequent negotiations. However, the
conflict is between rival organisations or departments, and
skilful negotiators never allow it to appear as conflict at the
personal level.

(2) There follows a period of informal negotiation, often
characterised by considerable personal friendliness and
agreement on common values (possibly quite irrelevant to the
negotiating issue). Both sides try to discover the other's
maximum and minimum objectives and to disentangle essential
differences and areas of agreement. Some informal agreement
about a possible solution may develop and even some ideas
about the stage management of the final formal bargaining.

(3) The negotiation concludes with further formal meetings
to reach a decision, where both parties again act as representatives of their organisation.

We have confirmation from experienced trade union and
management negotiators that they rely heavily on friendly,
informal, behind-the-scenes negotiations, and also that on
occasion the final formal agreement is carefully stage-
managed in advance. This is primarily to ensure that both
sides retain credibility with the groups they have to represent.
A time deadline is detrimental to this bargaining, since it
pushes one side or the other towards a compromise or a
capitulation for the sake of short-term objectives.

APPLICATION TO NEGOTIATING WITH COLLEAGUES

These findings, if put together, suggest a strategy for negotiating with colleagues:

(1) The manager should decide his objectives. In particular, he should decide his ideal solution, the most he would like and also the least he could accept. He must deal with his colleagues within these boundaries.

(2) He should consider the arguments in support of his case and gather as much evidence as possible to support it. He should ensure he is aware of its weaknesses, know the facts involved, and develop some counter arguments.

(3) He should decide who are the principal negotiators with whom he has to deal and try to ensure that he negotiates directly with them and not with others who ultimately cannot decide the issue.

(4) He should ensure that he maintains, as far as possible, good personal relationship with the negotiators (colleagues) with whom he usually has to deal.

(5) He should determine as far as possible where he must try for a share of limited resources and where he can offer a collaboration which might extend the total resources of both parties. He should use his imagination to extend these areas of collaboration.

Other points relate to the tactics he might adopt in discussion. They suggest he should:

(1) State his department's needs clearly and forcibly at the outset.

(2) Ask questions which help him to understand his colleagues' maximum and minimum requirements.

(3) Listen for information which will indicate where he can help or collaborate to enable both sides to obtain their objectives.

(4) Be prepared to concede, at a strategic moment, on non-essential issues.

(5) Try always to remain friendly on a personal level, without conceding the needs of his department.

(6) Try to understand the colleagues' point of view and difficulties without abandoning representation of his own department.

(7) Try never to settle for a poor compromise because of extraneous pressures.

(8) Work towards agreement which satisfies his colleagues' needs as well as his own.

(9) Try to maintain a consistent style with all colleagues, since this will enable them to respond more effectively.

(10) Be prepared to help 'stage-manage' a deal, so that each side's objectives are ostensibly met.

It is wise to confirm verbal agreements in writing. It is also essential to distinguish between bargaining in a role capacity and personal relationships. One manager was so surprised, for example, at some tough negotiating from a colleague that he complained, 'But you've always seemed so friendly!'

DEFINITION OF ROLES AND RESPONSIBILITIES: BEING
A SUBORDINATE

The assumption usually is that the definition of the roles and responsibilities of a subordinate should be provided by the superior, and that the subordinate who lacks a definition is entitled to grumble, exploit the situation or resign as he pleases. More constructively, he is certainly entitled to ask for such a definition, and he must take up, and if necessary develop, opportunities to see his superior regularly. The role the boss requires of a subordinate has to be understood, and can be learned only by meeting him. It may also be important for the subordinate to clarify the purpose of a meeting where the boss does not. Thus, one subordinate asked his superior why he had never given him the regular appraisal interview specified by company policy. The superior looked hurt and answered, 'But I did! Don't you remember that time we travelled home on the bus together?'

144

Only from regular meeting can the manager learn his boss's strengths and weaknesses and thus work to draw on the strengths and compensate for any limitation. With a respected boss, these are reasonable requirements. A special problem arises when the manager works for someone he cannot like, or possibly more serious, cannot respect. The temptation to by-pass such a superior should be resisted, as in the long run it is rarely in anybody's interests. The manager should continue to maintain as much communication as possible, and try to ensure that feelings of dislike are not being promoted by his own manner and behaviour. He should make a continuous positive effort to see and use any good qualities the superior may have.

Another sort of problem boss is the one who listens carefully to a case and apparently agrees to some solution, only to issue subsequently one that is markedly different. A well-known tycoon was particularly notorious for this type of behaviour. One subordinate who dealt with him successfully took to dictating a memorandum of the discussion immediately after every interview, adding a note that he was acting in accordance with this arrangement forthwith. He made sure that a copy of this record was on the tycoon's desk within the hour.

Information on working circumstances—work and standards of performance

BEING A SUPERIOR

A superior must provide a subordinate with general guidance, regular information and instruction about work, work objectives and standards, and the relationship of the work to the overall objectives of the concern. According to level, this type of information may need to be given daily, weekly, monthly, etc. He should ensure as far as possible that every subordinate knows the answers to the questions, 'What is my job?', 'Who is my boss?', 'How am I getting on?'

The implementation of this principle begins firstly with the

K   145 provision of a comprehensive set of written procedures for the reception and induction of newcomers. These should provide information concerning physical surroundings and conditions of service and an introduction to the people he will be working with—especially to his immediate superior and, if necessary, subordinates. Many firms provide regular induction programmes, lasting for half a day or longer; most firms have a written works handbook describing the official procedures. Secondly, each newcomer needs a written copy of his job description informing him of his duties, responsibilities and limits of discretion. Thirdly, managers need to be supported by a company system for the regular appraisal of staff, which is geared to policies for manpower planning and promotion and providing channels for systematic career development. Appraisal schemes provide the means for updating and agreeing job descriptions, for the agreement about performance standards, and for identifying training needs. This process goes on informally all the time, and in small concerns these *ad hoc* discussions may be all that is needed. But in larger concerns this process needs to be standardised if it is to be fair to every individual. In Chapter 4 we discussed appraisal systems and the interviewing skills required to run them.

Written procedures and documents such as these aid the manager but they cannot take the place of personal supervision. It is by working with the newcomer that the supervisor conveys the values, attitudes and expectations which are not in any job description, but which often spell success or failure. Many comments on a newcomers' failures relate to this aspect of their work: e.g., 'He does what he's told, but I can't get him to take that bit of extra responsibility.' 'I said, "Use a bit of initiative, but I didn't mean go off and order five hundred extra without consulting me".' Similarly, new procedures often involve new attitudes to work and change relationships which are not dealt with in the instruction manuals. The value of the example set by the manager himself should not be underestimated. He embodies the values described in the training situation since he is concerned to maintain his technical skill and, more broadly, to understand the goals and objectives of his section and their relation to company objectives.

The acquisition of job knowledge and preparation for further responsibilities must be integrated into the general work and life experience of the individual. It is ineffective to train a person in some skill, technique or area of knowledge and return him to a work environment where his new ability is manifestly not required or rewarded. This outcome is prevented when training is selected for the individual as a result of studying his work performance or the needs of his department. It is, however, rather likely to arise when training programmes are conceived by a central training department and put out to the rest of the company in a spirit of touting for custom. Thus in one course run by central training in a very large organisation, when students were asked how the course subject could be applied in their work one man replied, 'I'm sorry but I can't see any point at all where what I've learned here can be applied in my work. I can't apply it now, I've never been in a job where it could apply and I don't expect ever to be in one.' This manager had in fact been sent on the course as a general boost to his morale and with the notion that the subject matter might interest and could hardly harm him!

Conversely, where training is related to work, clearly linked to performance and to personal advancement, it becomes for many employees an important source of satisfaction at work. Even in the absence of appropriate company policies, the individual manager can do a good deal to foster this atmosphere in his own department. He needs to analyse a subordinate's training requirements and agree with the individual why he should train. Later he should help him to evaluate and apply what he has learned. One supervisor in charge of a group of semi-skilled operators explained how he tackled the problem. 'We'd gone training mad. I couldn't see the point of half of it.

We had everybody sent off on courses in every direction. I wasn't consulted—they just got sent. Then I started calling a meeting about once a month at which I always asked about the courses people had been on. I'd say, "Now Alf, you went on such and such a course last week. What did you get out of it? Can we apply it in our section?" Sometimes they could and sometimes they couldn't. Anyway, I passed their opinions to the departmental manager. Gradually he began to ask me about who should go where and we now see the point of training in our section.'

With more senior subordinates, day-to-day instruction is likely to be replaced by regular discussions agreeing work objectives. The more senior person is particularly likely to be concerned to see the relation of the sections work to the organisation as a whole, and all subordinates need to understand company fortunes and policy decisions as they affect their work and working conditions.

BEING A COLLEAGUE, BEING A SUBORDINATE

Written procedures for the induction of staff, job descriptions and an appraisal system contribute as much towards effective relationships between colleagues as they do for superiors and subordinates. Equally, the system should provide regular procedures for keeping colleagues informed about each others' activities—both present work schedules and background information. Accepting personal responsibility for maintaining these systems is an important part of being an effective colleague. A newly-appointed head of a busy headquarters department suddenly surprised all his colleagues by a series of irritable demands to be 'kept in the picture'. The incidents he complains about were discussed and procedures agreed for keeping him informed and ensuring his prior agreement henceforth. It was also agreed that certain responsibilities for organising relevant activities should be handed over to his department forthwith. It was soon discovered, however, that

148

it was impossible to keep him informed, obtain his agreement and so forth, as he was almost never in his office. He was frequently visiting units of the organisation and had neglected to develop adequate delegation and communication channels. Within six months he was forced into another meeting at which colleagues demonstrated—some of them with enthusiasm—that attempts to meet his requirements had resulted in constant delays and impediments in work which had previously proceeded smoothly. He was the only one, they pointed out, who had failed in implementing the revised procedures designed to meet his needs.

Good personal relationships are likely to ensure that background information, enough to explain the manager's working circumstances, reaches the appropriate people. The manager should also help communication by developing regular procedures for supplying work information to colleagues who need it.

The superior's need for information is comparable, except that he usually relies upon his subordinate to filter information so that it relates to his own wider responsibilities. Sometimes, as in writing a report (Chapter 3) it may be part of the manager's job to justify demands upon a superior's time by explaining why some information is relevant. The temptation to suppress unwelcome information, when reporting to a superior, is strong. It may well be advantageous in the short term for the individual subordinate to suppress such news, particularly if it could reflect upon his own efficiency. However, the resulting problems often accumulate and may have serious consequences. Regular reporting systems offer the best protection against this sort of situation. The manager should aim to present essential information frequently and objectively (e.g., in the form of accounts, sales records, etc.) and so ensure that trends are discussed before they reach traumatic proportions.

Equally, colleagues and superiors depend on an individual manager consistently to maintain acceptable standards of work. He is considerably helped in this by regular monitoring from his own superior and by relationships friendly enough to ensure understanding of the cause of any deviation. Unfortunately, good working standards from colleagues and superiors are often taken for granted. It is the deviation from good performance which attracts sharp critical attention. The consistently good performance which contributes so much to others' effectiveness and ease of work may earn general liking and respect but not, apparently, specific praise and reward. This problem of unbalanced criticism is illustrated in an unpublished survey of staff performance review-forms undertaken at Esso Fawley Refinery. The appraisers were required to rate subordinates on various personality traits on a five-point scale. The scale presupposed a normal distribution curve. Ratings, however, showed a skewed distribution with 92 per cent of the rates scoring average or above. By contrast, the appraisers' comments which accompanied the ratings showed an average of seven times as many adverse observations as points for commendation. The precise, adverse attention given to unexpectedly poor performance may also threaten a friendly personal relationship just at the moment when it is most needed.

The best solution to this problem again seems to lie in more regular and constructive monitoring of performance which foster a precise awareness of each colleague's positive contribution as much as any shortcomings and which reveal any changes in performance at an early stage. Regular meeting between colleagues, and subordinates and superior, especially if planned as problem-solving meetings, can help with this.

Representation—relationships with other departments and the outside world

BEING A SUPERIOR, A COLLEAGUE AND A SUBORDINATE

Superiors are expected to represent the needs of their subordinates to their superiors or to colleagues of equal status.

Subordinates are sometimes required to fight with their superior for the interests of their group (sometimes as the unofficial spokesman) or for themselves. A leader who fails to support his team against hostile outside threats or who fails to obtain the best possible terms for them (compatible with the needs of the task or the organisation as a whole) forfeits the respect of his subordinates. It is not always agreeable to continue to argue forcefully for one's department against a hostile superior. Occasions arise when a manager may feel that in doing so he is putting his job, or at least his further advancement, on the line. The risks are real, but it is equally certain that the well-being of the organisation may depend upon managers courageous enough to take such risks. It is also apparent that, if some organisations and superiors penalise subordinates for continued strong representation of their department's cause, others recognise this ability and will reward it.

A manager can be helped to do an honest and competent job of representation by the way his concern organises his work and his position in the hierarchy. His position can be protected while he fights for necessary but unpopular causes. Communities and occupations which make great demands on their members (religious orders, para-medical services, etc.) are often distinguished by the care they take to ensure that individual unselfishness does not result in the person losing status. By means of uniforms, regulations, habitat, etc., they ensure that the individual's special standard of service can be acknowledged by us all.

Similarly some organisations go some way towards recognising this type of contribution from their managers. The status symbols which help more obviously self-denying groups can help managers also. A job title, good office accommodation and adequate professional assistance are testimonies to offset self-abnegating behaviour. It may also be possible positively to reward managers prepared to devote time to others' advancement. A small but important example is the performance appraisal system which specifically requires the appraiser to note how successful the individual manager has been in developing his own subordinates.

The manager can also help himself by developing appropriate skills to aid him in carrying out this representative role. Representation calls particularly for skill in persuading and in making a case (described in Chapter 3). However, in many situations the manager may well need to press the case of his department or fight for its needs to the point of threatening his own personal position. What is he to do? He should of course be able to take comfort in the fact that improved setting of objectives and recording of results should mean that his successful resolution of an issue is increasingly likely to be observed. But whether or not these records are available, he can also take positive steps to ensure that his contribution is recognised. Self-presentation is one of the skills of management and can be likened to the marketing of any product.

Self-presentation depends, as do so many aspects of successful management, on the presenter himself being present. It is possible to be represented by the written word or by deputies. But a manager interested in self-presentation should take time to be known to others, particularly to the influential amongst his subordinates, his peers and the company leaders. Many of the ways in which we present ourselves have been perceptively analysed by Goffman. Dress and grooming are important and possibly even more important in management, are manner and bearing. People used to authority are likely to convey this fact by posture and expression. They remain in an upright though easy posture when talking to subordinates. They smile pleasantly rather than excessively. The subordinate is more likely to lean forward; his expression and posture often suggest someone less conscious of his dignity, more concerned to please.

The behaviours of superior people are unconsciously copied by others on promotion until by the time a junior becomes a senior he has generally acquired 'quite naturally'

152

the dress and bearing of a person of status. It has become clear, without anything being said, that he tends to expect and receive deference from others. Although this process is normally unconscious, copying can also be conscious and still be effective. Experiments have shown that a person consciously copying some dominant pose is able to influence others to treat him more deferentially. A number of changes occur when someone is accepted as being of high status. A further finding from studies of negotiating behaviour stresses the different reception accorded to the claims of groups of high and low status. High-status people are listened to, low-status people are usually assumed to be raising some parochial grievance.

So a first step in self-presentation is to take the trouble to be there, and a second is to ensure that dress, grooming and manner convey the impression required and encourage others to respond appropriately. The manager must try to see that his credentials are publicly known. Although he cannot go on stating them himself he should take care to do so on appropriate occasions. A salesman going to a new territory should ensure that he himself is sold in advance and a newcomer to a job should think of indirect ways of indicating his expertise. The most attractive way of doing this, of course, is to put any special skill and knowledge at the service of a colleague, for example, in helping to solve a problem. Conversely, the wise self-presenter who has little to contribute keeps quiet about the fact, avoids being in situations where his ignorance will become obvious and learns as fast as he can.

People who intend to attain positions of influence behave in predictable ways. They 'professionalise' their work, gradually dropping the menial aspects and accepting any opportunities for more difficult and responsible tasks. They may also gradually establish protective conditions for their work—improved physical surroundings, more assistants, fewer people entitled to give them orders. Their assistants,

too, become more professional. One young manager emphasised his own status to an interviewer as follows:

> *Q*. 'How many people work for you?'
> *Manager*. 'I have one assistant.'
> *Q*. 'Oh, I see, a sort of clerk?'
> *Manager*. 'He does a clerk's job but he's a graduate. My
> assistants have always been graduates.'

People seeking seniority also tend to work through lieutenants.
They usually ensure that they are well known to everyone in
the group they supervise, but they know the official and the
unofficial leaders in that group and are careful to transmit
orders and comments through these people. The manager who
seeks advancement can note these behaviours and may decide
to copy them. It must also be remarked, however, that they
incur considerable irritation from colleagues and superiors if
the behaviours are not matched by real competence and a
willingness to help maintain the high standards of the group
as a whole.

The points which help a speaker to win over an audience
can all also help the manager to gain friends and status. He
is helped by a friendly interest in people, with the proviso
that he must retain a slight distance from subordinates. He
is helped by a reputation for sincerity, which in practice
usually seems to mean a way of behaving towards others that
is consistently sustained. He is helped if he has manifestly
attractive attributes such as health, looks, vitality and stamina,
or admired qualities, such as brains, creativeness, humour,
enthusiasm, physical and moral courage and kindliness. A
surprising amount of mileage can be made out of expertise in
particular sports. We have often been told that a particular
director 'got a blue', 'played for England', etc., as though
these were obvious credentials for governing a company. The
increasing professionalism of management is, of course,
tending to reduce the influence of these irrelevant qualities.
But if they are allied to an ability to do the job, they remain

powerful assets. The manager who wants to protect and advance himself whilst doing an honest professional job can usefully study his self-presentation just as one other aspect of his total task, and find ways of publicising and capitalising on all his assets.

MANAGING THE TRADE UNION SITUATION

The manager plays both a leadership and representative role in relation to the Trade Unions and in particular to his own shop stewards or worker representatives. It has been aptly said that a manager gets the shop steward he deserves. A wise manager therefore builds structures and uses skills which encourage positive contributions from workers. He recognises that Trade Unions representatives have a positive role to play, he encourages his staff to join and take an active part in a Trade Union, ensures his shop steward is trained for his role, affords him facilities and informs and consults him. The manager also builds and maintains a friendly relationship with the local Trade Union official. By thus taking the initiative the manager is in the best position to guide and control the Trade Union situation.

RESEARCH EVIDENCE AND THEORIES ABOUT
MOTIVATION

The practical steps outlined in this chapter and in Chapter 7 relate to current theories of motivation which offer a systematic way of considering human needs and the extent to which they are, or can be, satisfied at work. These theories, based on research which is still proceeding, place greater emphasis than in the past on managers working constantly to understand and to cater for the needs of their staff for recognition, for advancement, for a satisfying and rewarding job and for the challenge of being fully used. A full description of these researches can be found in the further reading suggested at the end of this chapter. They serve as background information and suggest where to look if matters seem to be going wrong. An attitude survey (of the sort conducted by The National Institute of Industrial Psychology) can yield a closer analysis of the motives and attitudes of a particular group of subordinates. But the manager's surest guide to understanding the individual will remain his own ability to listen and observe.

Action points

1. Examine and, if necessary, redefine and reorganise the structure which affects individual roles and role relationships between subordinates, colleagues and superiors.

2. Examine and, if necessary, reorganise policies and procedures for the selection, induction and continuing training of staff.

3. Introduce and maintain an effective appraisal scheme.

4. Maintain and keep open systematic channels of communication with subordinates, colleagues and superiors.

5. Learn the skills of negotiating, bargaining, persuading interviewing and representation (including self-representation).

6. Ensure that everyone at each level has his own targets within the overall objective of the enterprise.

7. Understand and make use of current knowledge about motivation.

Further reading

General books dealing with this subject are:

Douglas McGregor, *The Human Side of Enterprise* (McGraw-Hill, New York, 1960)

Roger Brown, *Social Psychology* (Free Press, New York, 1965)

Joseph Tiffin and E. J. McCormick, *Industrial Psychology* 3rd ed. (Allen & Unwin, 1968)

The skills of negotiating are dealt with in:

Leonard Sayles, *Managerial Behavior* (McGraw-Hill, New York, 1964)

I. E. Morley and G. M. Stephenson, 'Strength of case, communication systems and the outcome of simulated negotiations. Some social psychological aspects of bargaining', *Industrial Relations Journal* (Summer, 1970)

The skills of self-presentation are described by:

Erving Goffman, *The Presentation of Self in Everyday Life* (Allen Lane, The Penguin Press, 1969)

Some effects of poor structures are covered in a research study entitled:

Robert L. Kahn etc., *Organisational Stress: Studies in Role Conflict and Ambiguity* (Wiley, New York, 1964)

Induction training:

W. R. Marks, *Induction. Acclimatizing people to work* (IPM Publications, 1970)

A survey of modern motivational theories and research can be obtained by reading:

A. H. Maslow, *Motivation and Personality* (Harper & Row, New York, 1970)

V. H. Vroom, *Work & Motivation* (Wiley, New York, 1964)

Frederick Herzberk, *Work and the Nature of Man* (World Publishing Co., New York, 1966)

David C. McClelland, *The Achieving Society* (Free Press, New York, 1967)

Michael Argyle, *The Social Psychology of Work* (Allen Lane, The Penguin Press, 1972)

7
BUILDING AND LEADING WORK GROUPS

Most work is done in groups. This is true of animals and primitive men throughout history, under widely differing technological and cultural conditions. Social groups, large and small, develop leadership hierarchies. Numerous laboratory experiments have shown how the members who are best at the task being performed become informal leaders. The other members do not necessarily like these people, but they realise that the group is more likely to reach its goals if the right people are in charge. Other studies have shown that group effectiveness depends on the development of a stable leadership hierarchy of this kind. In small social groups with no appointed leader it is often found that *two* unofficial leaders emerge: one is a 'task leader' who takes decisions about how the work is to be done, the other is the 'socio-emotional leader' who looks after the welfare of the group members. However, in most working groups there is one appointed leader, and he is expected to do both jobs. On the one hand, he has to allocate the work, show people how to do it and make sure they do it properly; on the other, he has to deal with individual problems, see that no one is unhappy or worried about the working arrangements and see that the group members get on well together. The socially-skilled leader of a working group is effective at both tasks, and is successful in generating both high productivity from the group and also a high level of job satisfaction, low absenteeism and low labour turnover.

So the successful leader of a work group has to look after both the *task* and the *group*—including both the welfare of individuals and their harmony as a team. Two behavioural scientists, Blake and Mouton, have translated

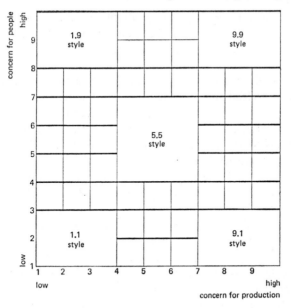

Fig. 7.1.

this theory into leadership terms for managers (see Fig. 7.1, from *The Managerial Grid*).

One dimension measures concern for people, the other concern for production.

> The 9.1 style concentrates on the task and ignores consideration for people.
>
> The 1.9 style has high consideration for people and values friendly relationships more than productivity.
>
> The 1.1 style has little concern for people or for production. It keeps the manager in a job and out of trouble.
>
> The 5.5 style is a compromise position. It aims to produce as much as possible while keeping people happy.
>
> The 9.9 style obtains high productivity *through* gaining commitment. It harnesses individual and group motivations to the common task.

Although the 9.9 style is usually superior, a leader can vary his style according to the requirements of the situation, as we shall see later in this chapter.

As well as first-line leaders, there have to be second-line leaders, to lead and coordinate the first-line leaders. The larger the working organisation, the more levels there have to be in the hierarchy. This will also depend on the span of control; if this is 10 at the bottom and 5 at higher levels, 250 workers require three levels of supervision; if it is 20 at the bottom level and 12 higher up, they will only need two levels In addition to higher levels of management there may also be staff managers dealing with finance, personnel and other specialised matters. This changes the position of line managers since some of their work is done for them, and they are less autonomous.

The organisation may be highly authoritarian, or it may delegate considerable authority to junior managers and supervisors. There may be joint consultative committees, on which shop-floor workers are represented; this can make the work of first-line leaders more difficult, since complaints about them can be referred to the committees, so that greater skill is needed in handling men. Most leaders are 'men in the middle', in that they face both upwards and downwards in the hierarchy, and experience role conflict as a result of conflicting social pressures. However, this problem is particularly acute for first-line leaders, since their subordinates tend to have low identification with the organisation, and are likely to combine together through the unions or joint consultative committees.

Managers at each level vary in their effectiveness. Research has been able to isolate the social skills of leaders of work groups which result in greatest productivity and satisfaction.

Research, too, has identified some of the major structural and organisational factors facilitating the effectiveness of groups to work together, and so making it easier for a leader to exercise the appropriate social skills.

160

In this chapter we shall consider first the structure and organisation of work groups, then the skills of leading and supervising face-to-face groups, and finally the different skills of second- and third-line leaders.

The structure and organisation of work groups

GROUPS FORM TO COOPERATE OVER WORK

Group members are often brought together through their cooperation over their various types of work. For example, one worker may need to finish a sub-assembly before the next one can start his job. Two men may need to move large sheets of steel into a press and then work the press together, or a group may complete a whole job (as in mining when a group cut the coal, fill and do stonework). In automated plants there may be links between people who have to communicate information to one another, possibly by remote control. Managers need to cooperate with fellow managers.

The very complexity of modern industry requires cooperative groups to accomplish work. For example, monitoring output of manufacturing or running an oil refinery or a research laboratory. Often no one man is expert enough to solve all the problems on his own.

ADVANTAGES OF STRONG, COHESIVE GROUPS

If these groups become strongly-knit, cohesive groups (or teams) many favourable results follow. Groups develop common norms (ways of behaving, attitudes and standards). Groups share norms on how fast and hard and to what standards members should work. They share attitudes towards managers, unions and other groups. They hold common beliefs (which may be quite mistaken) about matters which are perhaps too complex for them to understand fully. Interpersonal behaviour is also regulated by group norms. To support these norms groups develop shared means of com-

L   161

Skills with people

munications such as a private slang terminology. Norms are also formed about clothes and other physical appearance aspects. Sayles and Strauss described how one of them conducted interviews in a factory. He usually wore a T-shirt to demonstrate his identification with the workers. One day he wore a shirt and tie and several workers immediately asked him, 'What's wrong—sold out to management?' Speech and clothes are such a declaration of group membership that even though in this case Sayles was not a true member of the group, his clothes had spoken a message of identification.

The more cohesive the group, the more individual members adhere to the norms. This may be very useful, since norms can sustain a high standard of work, etc. However, norms can also work in the opposite direction to restrict output. But provided a manager leads his group skilfully to a shared goal using the social skills described in this chapter, the norms will be helping his subordinates to remain solidly behind him as a group.

Members of cohesive groups talk more to each other, cooperate more and then job satisfaction is greater. They also resist frustration more. In one experiment, people who had contact with each other argued more aggressively with a restrictive supervisor than did other people who kept on their own. Similar results were obtained in an experiment with Dutch shopkeepers threatened with the information that a super-market was going to open in their town. Teams help each other more and many studies have found that labour turnover and absenteeism are less in cohesive groups. The study in coalmining described shows how absenteeism and labour turnover fell after the introduction of the modified longwall method. In a textile situation, although the workers felt hostile to the company as a whole, groups with a strong-capacity group spirit had less labour turnover than those which did not.

Productivity is not always higher in cohesive groups, though it usually is when the task requires a great deal of helping or coordination. Some researches support this conclusion. Katz and Kahn found that the foremen of 60 per cent of high-output sections in a heavy engineering factory described their men as good at helping each other, compared with 41 per cent in low-output sections. Results from studies of groups in clerical work and railroad maintenance crews showed that work groups with greater pride in their production, or with feelings of greater loyalty to the group, were often the groups producing at high level. Perhaps these many favourable aspects follow because a cohesive group gives satisfaction to its individual members, and because social interaction is easier and the group members help one another and cooperate more. Attraction to the group may also be based on the prestige of belonging to it, the high pay, or the challenge of the work, as well as the interpersonal attraction of membership.

The sense of worth is increased by the many different roles which people play in such a group. Individuals prize their reputation as the humourist, the helpful member, the task leader or the popular leader. Other necessary roles may be divided between different group experts, for example, one may know about trade union matters, and another about welfare facilities.

DISADVANTAGES OF COHESIVE GROUPS

Strong, cohesive groups bring considerable advantages to the work situation. They can, however, use their power to work against the manager's objectives. For example, since strongly knit, cohesive groups keep closely to their norms, if the group has settled for low-output norms production will suffer more from such a group.

Again, attitudes towards outside groups can become hostile, with a resulting lack of cooperation. New members can have difficulty in feeling accepted. Possibly the most dangerous and damaging effect is that such groups seek to continue in being, and resist any changes which threaten their existence. Research groups, for example, may start a new project, not for its intrinsic value, but because it keeps the group together. Committees can continue to meet long after their usefulness is over.

In the following section we consider the conditions for fostering strong, cohesive work groups. It is the manager's leadership skills which will determine whether these groups work effectively for his objectives.

HOW ARE STRONG COHESIVE GROUPS ORGANISED?
TECHNOLOGY

In some industries powerful groups are created by the technology; in others the reverse is true.

A steelworks before automation is an example of the former. Chadwick-Jones found that crews needed a high degree of coordination to complete a cycle, and jobs were interchangeable between operatives. If men fitted into the team well they received a number of rewards in the form of additional relief breaks and increased variety through exchange of tasks. The technology determined the way the group was formed and this in turn led to a common insistence of 'harmony' and a deep feeling of team spirit amongst the men, who frequently described the works as 'home'. Every man's job in the mill was seen to be 'important'. Crews chose each other and men knew they could progress up the skill ladder with age. Crew members were firm friends, drank at the same pubs outside work and visited each other at home.

Other types of technology breed weak groups. In the study by John Goldthorpe and his colleagues of craftsmen, setters, process workers, machinists and assemblers in a motor-car factory, the researchers found 'there was no occupational group or sub-group (amongst those studied) where conditions prevailed which were entirely favourable for the creating of solid work groups'. Of the tool makers it could be said that technical organisation *permitted* groups to form; with other work groups the technology activity *prevented* groups from developing. The assembly line, for example, permitted a man to have a conversation with his immediate neighbours, but prevented a common network of relationships from developing. Only 22 per cent reported talking a 'good deal' to their work mates. Relationships appeared to be superficial; 45 per cent had no close friends at work, 65 per cent said it would not bother them much to be moved.

Similarly, when the steelworkers described earlier moved to a new automated plant, continuous flow treatment of steel created a majority of jobs of a routine monitoring type. These called for a high degree of responsibility, but were low in 'difficulty'. The rich social contacts of the old team system gave way to 'sparse' communications on the flow-process line. Less commitment was required to team exchanges and relationships, and less support to other individuals was offered. The technical reorganisation had disrupted and impoverished the old system of group interactions.

Managers, therefore, can consciously structure cohesive work groups by building technical systems which encourage (or at least permit) a strong group or team to form. Chadwick-Jones suggests, for example, that the new process 'flow' steel plant should have been examined at the design stage, and the new technical processes set up in ways which would have preserved as much of the old group loyalties as possible. The men studied by Goldthorpe were frequently moved round by management. This increased their inability to form stable interpersonal relationships. This is such a common practice amongst managers that Elton Mayo was able to state, 'We are technically competent, as no other age in history, and we combine this with utter social incompetence.'

With the use of some creative imagination, managers could significantly transform even the most socially unpromising technological circumstances. Examples of this come from the work of the Tavistock Institute of Human Relations described in Chapter 8. A modified organisation for coal-getting combined the new technology with the old social structure. As a result, team spirit revived, men were happier and production rose considerably. A similar example comes from the assembly line at a light engineering factory. On a long assembly line morale and job satisfaction were low. One girl expressed a general feeling when she said, 'It is dreadful working in such a large group; I should love to work in a small group.' The nature of the work permitted one such group to exist in the department. Five other such groups were created artificially by dividing one long assembly line into five parts, with stocks in between each. Follow-up studies showed that the girls on the small line were a happy, closely-knit group. They saw the result of their work and were paid on a group-bonus scheme. The groups created by the management were the next happiest in that department, their job satisfaction was higher and they felt a greater sense of belonging, although they still felt they belonged to the larger assembly line group.

The researchers concluded that the first small group had probably derived the fullest benefits because they saw their own end product. The next best arrangement was smaller groups with intervening spaces, especially if the spatial arrangements could increase the feeling of cooperation.

A SHARED COMMUNICATION SYSTEM, WORK PLACE, BONUS

Not all work groups, however, come together because of a common task. Some groups become cohesive because of a shared communication system. Research has demonstrated that workers in close proximity to each other, in the same room or in the same section of an office, are presented with the opportunity of becoming closely-knit cohesive groups. Geography is a powerful instrument. One piece of research on a housing site for married students showed that friendship patterns followed the positioning of apartments. Most families made the majority of their friends in their own buildings and, in particular, on their own floor. The couples with the most friends occupied a strategic position on the ground floor nearest the building's entrance. Couples physically isolated were also socially isolated and least liked. Similarly, workers concentrated in one place doing the same job were one of the strongly-knit types of group found by Sayles in a study made within 30 factories and 300 work groups.

If workers also share a common supervisor, or a common group bonus, their feelings of identification with each other become the stronger. Some managers have studied their groups from this point of view and created communication structures where none existed naturally. One firm fostered the sense of belonging amongst their long-distance lorry drivers by building a rest-room where they could meet each other at the head depot. Another firm overcame some of the secretaries' resistance to changing from an individual secretarial system to a typing-pool system by providing a well-furnished rest-room where they could meet at tea breaks as a group.

Another highly-integrated group, studied by Sayles and Strauss, never saw each other on the job, yet by means of a telephone linkage dominated the union and won substantial wage increases for themselves. An earlier enquiry made by Elton Mayo, while lacking the rigorous control of later studies, shows the importance of creating cohesive groups. After making a study of a male spinning department, where extremely high labour turnover was occurring, Elton Mayo introduced rest periods to reduce fatigue. The men then decided *in groups* how these pauses should operate. As a result, productivity improved and labour turnover fell dramatically. Mayo thought that this was due to physical improvements, but perhaps more importantly to the transformation of the men from a 'horde of solitaries' into a social group responsible for organising rest pauses and using these for communication and interaction.

In a study of twenty-five Lancashire hospitals Professor R. W. Revans discovered that the speed of recovery of patients was affected by the existence or non-existence of a communication system between medical consultants, matron, sisters, nurses and probationers. In hospitals where consultants and

167

the matron discussed matters with the ward sisters and welcomed their suggestions, the ward sisters were more likely to communicate with their nurses and student nurses, who in turn were encouraged to talk and listen to the patients. The hospital with a good communication system had not only a stable professional staff (the wastage rate of nurses, student nurses and ward sisters was low) but also enabled its patients to recover more rapidly. In other hospitals the position was reversed. The ward sisters felt isolated and unsupported. In one hospital, for example, the sisters' opinions were so discouraged by the consultants that one said, 'We are not fighting death here, but the doctors.' In these hospitals patients took longer to recover and the staff wastage-rate was high.

SIZE

Research shows that the strength of group feelings varies with size. It is easier to feel a sense of belonging to a group containing five to ten members. A number of experiments have shown that smaller groups do better at a variety of tasks, and the rates of absenteeism and labour turnover can be three or four times as great in larger groups. Similar results were found by the Acton Society Trust, investigating absenteeism and accidents in relation to size in the coal industry, a large industrial group and a retail store. Absenteeism and accident rates were much greater in the larger pits, factories and stores. Marriott found that the relative output of 239 workers in two automobile factories was generally greater in small groups of ten to fifteen than in large groups of fifty.

The traditional rule was that the span of control of a chief executive should not be more than about seven, and that of a first-line supervisor not more than about twenty. It has been found in the American firm Sears Roebuck, however, that a very high span of control is possible, since store managers have a large degree of autonomy, and coordination between stores is largely achieved by computer.

COMPATIBILITY OF MEMBERS

Groups can also be composed so that people who are alike, or think alike in some way, are put together. Age, sex, race, attitudes, interests and friendship patterns can all be taken into account. When the teams at the cash-out desk in an American supermarket were gradually sorted into homogeneous groups of this type, both their efficiency and job satisfaction began to rise. In another firm, skilled workers selected their first, second and third choice for a working partner. After some months, friction had been practically eliminated and turnover dropped from 3·11 per cent to ·27 per cent. Labour and material costs dropped and there was an overall saving in production costs.

Conversely, groups will not develop permanently satisfying relationships where the members are simply not compatible. Several experiments in which incompatible people have been put in groups (for example, some members high in dominance, or with a low need for making relationships) have demonstrated that these groups were ineffective at tasks requiring cooperation. Again, groups of four were set up with an authoritarian leader and democratic followers or vice versa. In these cases, satisfaction was lower, communications suffered, conflicts rose and cooperation fell.

ROLE CONGRUENCE

Another consideration when composing groups, is whether or not all the roles an individual has to play are of similar status. A person should not have high status in the group in one respect and low status in another. An example of this and its effects comes from the study made by W. F. Whyte in Chicago restaurants (described on p. 110). The waitresses and the cooks had many arguments, which Whyte decided was caused by the high-status cooks taking orders from the low-status waitresses. Relationships improved when the

169

waitresses put their orders on to a spindle from which the cooks took them and attended to them at their own convenience.

PERMANENCE

It takes time for groups to grow. B. W. Tuckman analysed a number of studies of group development and found they typically went through four stages:

(1) forming, when they discover the task and the rules of the work;

(2) storming, when they resist the demands of the job or argue with each other and rebel against leadership;

(3) norming, when they exchange views and feelings and cooperation begins to develop;

(4) performing, when solutions begin to emerge and attempts to complete the task are made.

This is the major work period; the group has grown to maturity. The time it takes to reach this stage appears to relate to the size of the group and to the complexity of its task. Some groups may take a year to reach full efficiency. It is important to allow time for this process and try not to disturb a group or alter its membership during its formation.

The effects of leadership skills

A manager can lay the foundations of a cooperative team by a careful design of its structure. The type of leadership he exercises will then determine whether or not the group will then attain its maximum effectiveness. A large amount of research has been carried out in this area of supervisory and leadership skills. The basic design of these studies is to compare the style of supervision of a number of supervisors in charge of high-producing groups with the style of supervision of those with low-output groups. We shall now consider, therefore, the range of productivity, etc., of essentially similar working groups, but with different kinds of supervision.

Output. The effect of supervision on output varies greatly under different conditions. Output here is usually measured in terms of the amount of useful work completed per hour, sometimes in time-study units. Likert reports a number of studies showing large differences in the productivity of similar departments whose supervisors used different styles of supervision. In one of these studies the productivities of different clusters of departments were 6, 40, 46 and 71 units respectively. However, the first cluster consisted of two departments which were very hostile towards their supervisors; the ratio of 40:71, or a 78 per cent increase, is still rather greater than has been found in most studies. The effects of supervision are much less than this where work is machine-paced.

Absenteeism. There is a rather closer relationship between absenteeism and supervisory behaviour. In the famous Relay Assembly Room at the Western Electric Company, absenteeism dropped during the course of the experiment to one-fifth of what it was before (one-third the rate for the rest of the factory), as did amount of illness and lateness. Other studies have obtained similar results.

Labour turnover. In one study a ratio of about 4:1 was found between turnover rates in departments whose supervisors differed in styles of supervision. However, the effect was most marked for the very worst supervisors (Fig. 7.2 (b)).

Job satisfaction. In the same study there was a ratio of about 8:1 in grievance rates, and this was not just for the worst supervisors (Fig. 7.2 (c) and (d)). In other studies job satisfaction has usually been measured by a questionnaire, with a series of items directed at different areas of satisfaction.

The effects of supervision are most marked on job satisfaction, absenteeism and labour turnover. These variables

171

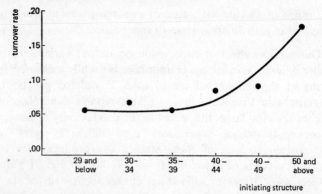

Fig. 7.2. (a)

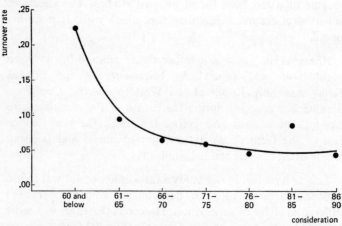

Fig. 7.2. (b) from Fleishman and Harris, 1962

are correlated together to some extent; absenteeism and turnover are economically important, especially when highly-skilled workers have to be replaced. The effects of supervision on output vary with the technology, and may be quite small in automated systems. On the other hand, supervision is a key variable when changes are made in working arrangements.

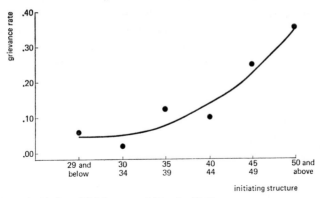

Fig. 7.2. (c) from Fleishman and Harris, 1962

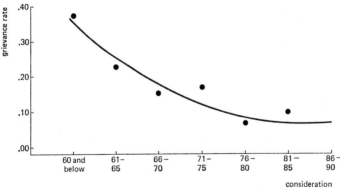

Fig. 7.2. (d) from Fleishman and Harris, 1962

How do supervisors behave?

Two dimensions of supervisory behaviour have been identified in studies of industrial and military groups. (1) Initiating structure, i.e. concern with the group task; and (2) Consideration, i.e. looking after the group members. These two dimensions equate with the 'task' and 'socio-emotional' concerns of the leader described earlier in this chapter. (3) A third dimension has been identified in other studies—the use of

Democratic-Persuasive social skills. This third factor provides the missing key to the first two: leaders who concentrate on production tend to upset the group unless they use a particular set of social skills; if they use participation and persuasion it is possible to deal with both task and group at the same time.

INITIATING STRUCTURE

There are a number of definite jobs which the foreman should do which are directly related to the task; these aspects of behaviour have been found to correlate together statistically, and have been named 'initiating structure'. These jobs include (a) planning and scheduling the work to be done, and making sure supplies are available, (b) instructing and training subordinates in how to do their work, (c) checking and correcting the work that has been done, (d) giving subordinates feedback on how well they are doing, and (e) motivating them to work effectively.

In a series of studies in different industrial settings by the Michigan group, it was found that productivity of work groups was higher when supervisors carried out these supervisory tasks, as opposed to working with the men, or doing routine jobs which could be delegated. On the other hand, output was usually higher under general rather than close supervision, and it looks as if too much initiating structure leads to a drop in output. It also leads to a drop in job satisfaction and labour turnover. The results of one study are shown in Fig. 7.2.

There is probably an optimum amount of guidance for any particular work group and type of task. The more highly skilled the subordinates, the less direction they need (as suggested by the Jaques time-span measure). Jaques found evidence that there is a relationship between an individual's pay and the interval of time before anyone checks up on his work (his 'time-span'). It may not be very clear just how much guidance is in fact given: Pelz found that the productivity of research workers was highest when they ostensibly had most freedom to do their own work, *but* saw the group supervisor every day.

'What goes on in these daily encounters? We are not sure, exactly; that is one of the areas that we are pushing further in our current studies. In all probability, the chief, by frequent enquiries, shows his interest in and enthusiasm for the work, and this is something on which a young scientist thrives. The chief may offer hints as to methods; he may refer to relevant articles; he may simply express his confidence in the progress that is being made. His very presence may serve as a motivating factor, causing the young scientist to push ahead as rapidly as he can, knowing that the chief will take pleasure in the results.' (Pelz: see further reading.)

There are special social skills associated with different parts of initiating structure, such as setting targets and appraising the results of work done. These skills were discussed in Chapters 4 and 5.

The work to be done by a supervisor on the task side depends on the range of men and equipment to be supervised and on the amount of authority and responsibility given to the supervisor. Supervision is an integral part of the socio-technical system. A field experiment was carried out in a military organisation for repairing and testing aircraft. Some supervisors were given responsibility for all aspects of the operation being supervised, including quality-control in some cases. This involved regrouping men and equipment and resulted in supervisors spending their time differently—more time on inspection, more time talking to their men about production and reporting to their own supervisors. Supervisors treated their men as a team, delegated responsibility for checking to craftsmen, rotated men between jobs and encouraged communication between section members. The result was an increase in quality, a reduction of costs, supervisors felt more autonomous and satisfied, and their men had greater job satisfaction.

These researches emphasise the modern approach to leadership. They show that it is not so much a mystique consisting of a set of *qualities* possessed by only a few favoured individuals, but rather that it is a function of the task and of the social skills used by people performing it.

CONSIDERATION (OR 'EMPLOYEE-CENTREDNESS')

The supervisor also had to look after the members of the group. This factor consists of (a) consideration of the needs of subordinates, helping them to attain rewards and avoid punishments, (b) establishing a warm and friendly supportive relationship with them, and (c) taking a personal interest in individuals, being understanding over mistakes, and dealing with inter-personal problems in the group. This kind of behaviour is not the opposite of production-centred behaviour, as was once supposed, but is independent of it.

A number of studies have found a correlation between consideration and productivity. This was found for railway maintenance gangs, for British electrical engineering workers, and in a variety of other settings. However, the size and also the direction of this relationship have been quite different in different studies, and it is not clear what the conditions are under which consideration affects output. A further problem is that the direction of causation may be the reverse of that assumed so far, i.e. supervisors may become more considerate when their groups work well. This is, however, opposed by one or two field experiments in which supervisors have been switched around.

A number of studies have shown that there is a strong relationship between consideration and job satisfaction, absenteeism and labour turnover. The effect on the last two variables is of the order 4:1 for supervisors at the upper and lower ends of consideration (Fig. 7.2). However, it is not enough for a supervisor to have good intentions; he must be sufficiently powerful to deliver rewards. Pelz has found that

there was a correlation between consideration and job satisfaction only for supervisors who were influential with their own
superiors.

DEMOCRATIC-PERSUASIVE SOCIAL SKILLS

The effective supervisor is found to use a set of social skills
which are not covered by the two dimensions considered so
far, but which are necessary in order to combine these dimensions successfully. There are three main components of these
skills: (a) motivating people by explanation and persuasion,
rather than just giving orders, (b) allowing subordinates to
participate in decisions that affect them, and (c) using techniques
of group discussion and group decision. There is extensive
evidence that supervisors using these skills are able to get
the group to set high targets, and to develop the motivation to
reach them, without themselves having to exert pressure.

A well-known experiment on these skills is Lippitt's work
with boys' clubs. Comparing democratically- and autocratically-led boys' clubs, he found that the democratic groups
worked just as hard when the leader was out of the room,
while the autocratically-led groups stopped work. Pelz, in his
study of research scientists, comments, 'We are becoming more
and more convinced that this active interest in the ongoing work,
combined with a hands-off policy concerning its direction, is
one of the most fruitful things a research chief can do . . .'

Other studies have found that when workers under piece-
work conditions are consulted, they often set higher targets
and enjoy the work more, while labour turnover is less. An
increase of 30–50 per cent took place in the rate of work by a
group of girls on a group bonus, who were allowed to control
the pace of their assembly-line belt. It is interesting that
participation in decisions affects productivity not only in the
USA, but also in Britain and in Japan. Democratic skills are
even effective in the army. It has been found that authoritarian
leadership in the American Army led to a high rate of going

M

AWOL, eating between meals, drunkenness, seeing the chaplain, blowing the top, fighting and sexual intercourse. On the other hand, a proportion of workers are quite happy with authoritarian leadership.

Allowing a group to participate in decisions involves the use of group-decision technique. It has long been realised that when a supervisor is dealing with the members of a cohesive group he is no longer dealing with a series of individuals, because the group has a greater influence on each person than he has. The supervisor must therefore deal with the group as a whole. The group-decision technique has three stages: (a) general discussion, intended to loosen the existing norm, and expose the diverse opinions held in the group, (b) persuasion by the leader, in the direction of a revised norm, and (c) bringing the group to decide in favour of the new goal, method, etc. Both laboratory and field experiments have shown the effectiveness of this technique, though this has been found to vary between different leaders. In an experimental analysis of the procedure it was found that the most important factors were the making of a group decision and the perception of unanimity in the group.

Why do democratic-persuasive skills affect productivity? There are a number of reasons. Participation leads to better decisions being made; those who take part in decision-taking become committed to the plan of action decided, and internalise the motivation to carry it out; and the increased discussion inside the group develops group cohesion and cooperation. If the democratic-persuasive style is so successful, why do so many leaders continue to be authoritarian, and believe this to be the best style? Likert suggests that since there is no correlation between productivity and job satisfaction, many supervisors may have realised this and put all their efforts into production, not bothering about their relationships with the men. And of course authoritarian supervisors *can* be effective, if combined with sufficiently heavy sanctions and efficient inspection—but at the cost of unhappy and unwilling workers, absenteeism and turnover, wastage of materials and a complete lack of everyday helpfulness and cooperation. During the Industrial Revolution this was a normal state of affairs, but under the changed industrial conditions of today it is extremely important to handle workers by more socially skilled methods.

Democratic-persuasive skills also affect the job satisfaction group of variables. Coch and French found no labour turnover in the group which participated in decisions in their field experiment, compared with 17 per cent in the others. In correlational studies it has often been found that workers who have more autonomy are more satisfied.

Variations in the optimum style of leadership

The results presented above show that, in general, leaders should (1) do the various jobs connected with the task, while avoiding 'close' supervision, (2) look after the welfare of individuals and the harmony of the group, and (3) do this in a democratic and persuasive manner. In practice, however, what the leader does will vary somewhat with the nature of the group, the technology and the problem being dealt with.

The most effective style of supervision varies in several ways with the technology and other variables. In craft work and unit production there are small and cohesive working groups; there is little need for supervision and no conflict between supervisors and working groups. In assembly-line and machine-tending work, groups are large, there is more use of machine-pacing and incentives, less close contact with supervisors, and the supervisor's behaviour has less influence. In more advanced technologies such as oil refineries and automated systems, there is a return to smaller groups, and better relations with supervisors. As yet, however, no systematic research has been done on how the most effective leadership style varies with the technology.

It has been found that the value of democratic-persuasive

179

skills varies considerably between different conditions. (1) Not everyone wants to take part in decisions; some would rather be told what to do. Vroom studied the participation of supervisors in higher decisions and found that there was a correlation of ·73 between participation and job satisfaction for those who had high independence needs and were low in authoritarianism; for those low in independence and high in authoritarianism there was no significant correlation. Similar findings were obtained for measures of their level of performance. (2) When it is necessary for rapid decisions to be taken, as in military or surgical operations, there is no time for discussion, though there can be participation in general planning. (3) When a group is large, participation becomes more difficult, the need for centralised control is greater and people accept such control more readily.

N. R. F. Maier suggests one useful rule which a manager can apply when deciding whether to involve his team in decisions. Decisions, he says, can be categorised in three main ways. The first type demands high-quality solution but low acceptance from the people involved. It is, for example, of critical importance to the continued success of a company that its directors should make correct decisions about launching into a new product or a new export market. Provided the order-book remains filled, however, most workers do not feel strongly about having a say in such matters. These types of decision are best made by the board.

The second type is about such matters as overtime rotas, holidays and seating arrangements. These require a high degree of acceptance from the people concerned but the quality of the decision is not very crucial from the manager's point of view. Hence these lend themselves naturally to a group-decision technique.

The third type of decision is one which requires both high quality and high acceptance. How the manager handles this depends on the forces in the actual situation, the forces in his group and the forces in himself. The group will be strengthened when the manager 'consults' or 'joins' his group in as many situations as possible, provided he uses the necessary skills to run such a meeting effectively (see Chapter 5).

Fiedler has obtained evidence that relative concern with group rather than task is successful under moderately 'favourable' conditions—i.e., when the supervisor is powerful, the group members like and respect him and the task is clearly structured. Under very favourable or unfavourable conditions he finds that the leader should concern himself more with the task. It may be necessary for a leader to use different styles at different stages of the task. We may add to this that there are times of crisis, for example with a near-bankrupt firm, when the needs of the task override the immediate needs of the people involved.

MIDDLE AND SENIOR MANAGERS

Above the first line of supervisors in the administrative hierarchy are second-line leaders; at the top of the hierarchy are more senior managers. The social skills needed by these two kinds of leader are different from those required by first-line supervisors, though all managers act as leaders of face-to-face groups composed of their immediate subordinates. It has been pointed out by a number of writers that the job to be performed and the skills required by second-line and senior managers are different from those of first-line supervisors. There have been a number of empirical studies of the jobs actually done by different levels of management.

Second-line leaders, unlike most supervisors, are part of management. They are trained for this and hope to have a career to higher levels. They need less technical expertise in the work of particular sections, and depend on supervisors and staff experts for guidance. They must understand the total picture of the particular parts of their own department, and how these fit in to the wider organisation, and know what area of freedom they have to operate in. Most of their work is with people and increasing demands on social skills are made at higher levels. In particular, they have to coordinate the activities of different sections and more of their communications are by telephone, letter or messenger. They are usually responsible for selection, training and setting standards, and for filling in the details of the plans made by more senior managers.

In order to make their particular contribution, senior managers need to be sensitive to external problems facing the organisation—external demands and opportunities, and changes in these. They need to be sensitive to internal pressures from individuals and sub-groups in the organisation and be able to integrate them. They need to be able to change the organisational structure in accordance with organisational goals, and to understand the working of social organisations.

Studies of communication in management hierarchies show special difficulties in communicating between different levels in the hierarchy. A manager often wants to communicate with people two or more levels below him. He has two main ways of doing this, neither of them very satisfactory. He can use the 'usual channels' of speaking first to his subordinates, or he can use letters, notices or the public address system. If he speaks through his immediate subordinates, at least four separate messages are needed before any feedback is received. There are liable to be various delays and distortions. The intermediate supervisors may reinterpret the instructions, or convey them with so little supporting information that 'research' has to be undertaken to find out what they are really about. Letters, etc., are faster and avoid distortion; however, there is no certainty that the information they convey has been received or understood. Such methods can be supplemented and improved by asking supervisors to reinforce them, or encouraging subordinates to discuss any problems with their immediate superiors.

While it is essential for senior staff to have fast and accurate information about how the work is going, difficulties encoun-

182

tered, etc., it is often very difficult for them to find out what is going on. Bad news is likely to be ill-received and may reflect the competence of the person who brings it; consequently, such information is delayed and distorted; supervisors and managers are told what they want to hear and when they are thought to be in a good enough mood to hear it. It has been found that upward communications are less accurate when subordinates are keen to be promoted. Although those at lower levels may be reluctant to report difficulties or lack of progress, they like to be consulted, to air their grievances, and to have their ideas heard at higher levels. In old-fashioned and authoritarian régimes this does not happen, and managers often create barriers to upward communication by isolating themselves in their offices. In more modern organisations better upward communication is achieved by suggestion schemes and appeals systems, representation on consultative committees, through trades unions and consultative styles of supervision.

There have been a number of studies of the effects of the supervisory styles of second-line leaders on productivity and job satisfaction. These studies show that second-line leaders have a greater influence on these variables than first-line leaders. A number of studies have shown that delegation and the use of participatory methods of leadership are very advantageous. On other dimensions different kinds of behaviour have been found to be most effective in first- and second-line leaders. It has been found that while first-line leaders in a nursing hierarchy should be high in initiating structure, second-line leaders should be low; consideration was related at both levels to the job satisfaction of subordinates and to ratings of leader effectiveness.

How do second-line and higher leaders affect subordinates two or more steps below them? In the first place they affect the style of supervision of first-line leaders by creating a climate in which their own leadership style is copied. Second-line leaders can also initiate and control training courses for first-line leaders. In addition, they are able to promote and select the kind of subordinates they think will be effective. They can modify the organisational structure to some extent, for example by greater delegation. And they can influence the whole department by setting standards of work. Thus a manager will succeed in building and maintaining a cooperative team, committed to a common objective, if he designs an appropriate structure for it and uses the general style of leadership and supervision we have described—consideration for the welfare of those concerned, attention to structuring the job and the use of the democratic style of leadership.

Appendix

Leadership is a universal institution stretching back into history and across all frontiers. We give below a short description of some of the lessons from the past and from other cultures.

In primitive societies work is done in small groups, whose leadership depends on the tribal hierarchy. In the Israeli kibbutz, leaders are elected and paid no more than others, but it is their job to supervise the work. In these cases all those concerned are directly motivated to do the work (gathering food, building houses, etc.), since it will immediately benefit them all.

The relationship between leaders and led has taken a variety of different forms in different cultures and historical periods. In the Roman Empire and other ancient civilisations, most work was done by slaves, who were brutally punished by their overseers if they did not work satisfactorily. In small households and estates the slaves were looked after in a more paternalistic way, but in the large farms and workshops they were found very difficult to handle because of their unwillingness. In the feudal period serfs worked for the lord of the manor because of a sworn obligation to do so, in exchange for which he provided protection and security. This system worked better than slavery, because of the high degree of acceptance of authority and the dependence on superiors for protection. A somewhat similar set of feudal, paternalistic relationships, with complete acceptance of hierarchical authority, is found in contemporary Japanese factories. In the early Industrial Revolution in England and Europe, unwilling workers were controlled partly by tyrannical discipline and fear of dismissal, partly by monetary rewards. The personnel practices of the later Industrial Revolution, became embodied in the writings of Fayol, Follett and others. and known as Classical Organisation Theory. This included the doctrines that there should be a high degree of division of labour and that workers should be motivated by economic incentives (controlled by fair discipline and impersonal rules and fitting into a pyramidal chain of command). In all these historical practices the task was achieved by the alternative use of force or cajolement—what has been described as the application of the stick or carrot.

These approaches were much criticised by social research workers of the 1940s and 50s who emphasised the importance of leadership skills, working groups and job satisfaction. They became known as the 'Human Relations Movement'. It was believed that happy workers would work harder, as would those who were supervised better and belonged to cooperative work groups. These ideas led to a great volume of empirical work and the results of social-science research became a factor which influenced management practices and the design of working organisations. For perhaps the first time in history, objective social research into the effects of different social arrangements became a factor bringing about social change. We have reviewed the research on the effects of supervision in this chapter. We have seen that research has gone considerably beyond earlier ideas, that the optimum style of leadership is a complex combination of social skills and that these vary with the technology and other features of the situation.

185

THE MODERN SITUATION

In modern societies, working groups are larger, technology more complex, and direct motivation to work is lacking and has to be replaced by other incentives. Informal groups are replaced by working organisations, where leaders are appointed to working groups usually from outside, and leaders have clear powers of reward and punishment over group members. In each case there is a definite social structure, in which there are institutionalised patterns of behaviour between leaders and led.

Individuals occupy definite positions in the social structure and they perform the roles associated with those positions—roles which have been worked out by earlier occupants. There is a certain amount of variation between individuals in how they play their roles, as a result of personality factors, but there are modul styles of behaviour, and occupants of positions are under some social pressure to conform.

In modern working organisations much use is made of impersonal mechanisms of control, such as automated and machine-paced equipment, and incentive schemes. This reduces the work to be done by leaders but they are still necessary to deal with changing conditions, to allocate jobs, to motivate and check, to create cooperation and avoid conflicts in the group, and to deal with the varied problems of individuals.

Points for a manager: practical actions building and leading work groups

1. Analyse the structure of the groups under his control and decide if the way these are organised will result in the maximum cohesiveness.

2. Decide whether the technology could be reorganised to increase group cohesiveness if the latter is weak.

3. Decide to restructure communication systems to increase group cohesiveness, if this is necessary.

4. Analyse the size and composition of groups under his control.

5. Decide to alter size of groups or the group membership if necessary.
6. Decide to keep group membership as permanent as is practicable.
7. Analyse his own leadership style.
8. Decide if he is doing all the leadership jobs required by the task, without too 'close' supervision.
9. Decide if he is paying sufficient attention to the welfare of individuals and the harmony of the group as a whole.
10. Determine when to work through individuals and when to use the group structure.
11. Decide to use a democratic-persuasive style as much as possible (bearing in mind its limitations).
12. Decide if he has changed his methods of leadership if a middle or senior manager to suit the requirements of these roles.

Further reading

The empirical studies referred to in this chapter are described in greater detail in:

> Michael Argyle, *The Social Psychology of Work* (Allen Lane, The Penguin Press, 1972)

An extensive review of the American research can be fixed in:

> V. H. Vroom, *Work and Motivation* (Wiley, New York, 1964)

The Michigan research is reported in:

> R. Likert, *New Patterns of Management* (McGraw-Hill, New York, 1961)

Two recent British studies of working groups are:

> J. K. Chadwick-Jones, *Automation and Behaviour* (Wiley Inter-science, New York, 1969)
> John H. Goldthorpe *et. al., The Affluent Worker* (Cambridge University Press, 1968)

An American study is described in:

> D. C. Pelz, 'Motivation of the engineering and research specialist,' *American Management Association General Management Series* **186**, 25–46 (1957)

8

INTERPERSONAL SKILLS AND
SOCIAL ENGINEERING

In laboratory studies it is possible to isolate the social skills required to achieve a particular objective. In the work situation, these skills are constantly modified, partly by the personalities involved, and considerably by the roles and relationships imposed on people by the work itself. In Chapter 3 we reviewed those aspects of personality which particularly affect communication between individuals. We also considered some of the prevailing influences which a working environment has upon attitudes and social interaction. In subsequent chapters it has usually been necessary to consider the effect of different social skills in relation to individual differences, and also to different work situations. In Chapter 7 it proved impossible to consider the application of recent research to the development of work teams without also considering some of the different work environments in which these teams may operate.

Though the social skills possessed by managers are extremely important, their exercise is influenced, changed or limited by the work environment. A continuous-flow process needs a different layout from that of an assembly line and so evolves a different social system, different patterns of interaction between individuals and different interpersonal skills. The supervision of a world-wide sales force, or of a remote copper mine far removed from the processing or distribution of the ore, creates problems of communication unknown to the management of a small homogeneous group all working in one room.

A considerable body of recent research has been concerned with the impact of technology upon social interaction at work. There is an increasing awareness that management is concerned with a socio-technical system and that new technologies often fail to yield their potential benefits because of their untoward effect on working relationships. There are also increasing signs that future managers will need to anticipate these effects and be prepared to adjust working methods to improve these patterns of interaction. The personal skills they require to build effective relationships with individuals and with groups will have to be matched by skills in social engineering.

This chapter reviews some of the research in this field and some of the imaginative experiments in social engineering which have already been undertaken. In our introductory chapter, we remarked on the curious fact that many managers still receive very little formal training in interpersonal skills, although these skills greatly affect the quality of their working contribution. In this chapter we set these skills in the working context. We believe that managers in the future will be trained not only in interpersonal skills, but also in an understanding of the need to provide social relationships at work which permit both effective technical operation and effective communication between people in the working community.

Socio-technical skills

The socio-technical system requires the people who work within it to possess several types of socio-technical skills. Little research has yet been done on the details of these skills, but two main categories may be distinguished—one concerning practical, and the other social relationships.

(1) Cooperation over a task
  (a) Parallel performance of similar tasks, e.g. independent assembly work, typing, research.
  (b) Cooperative performance of similar tasks, e.g. two-handed sawing, two to three men handling sheet steel in a press shop.
  (c) Cooperative and simultaneous performance of different but complementary tasks, e.g. pilot and navigator of a plane.

189

(d) Sequential performance of different but complementary tasks, e.g. assembly-line work, the different
jobs in coal-mining, etc.

(2) Social Relationships include:

(a) Conveying items of information.

(b) Discussion, as members of cooperative problem-
solving group.

(c) Negotiation, where there is some conflict of interest.

(d) Providing expert advice, without authority.

All these socio-technical skills call for the performer to be
motivated to influence the *others' social responses* and to emit a
continuous stream of *social initiatives and responses*. These
the performer continuously corrects as the result of *feedback*,
which he must *perceive* and relate to *appropriate corrective
action*.

Several of these different socio-technical skills can be seen
in the socio-technical system of a large restaurant, as described
by one research worker (Whyte) though the 'technology' here
is very simple.

The organisation of a large restaurant is shown in Fig. 8.1.
Here we can see the following types of interaction:

(1) parallel behaviour—waitresses;

(2) cooperative performance—cooks;

(3) cooperative and complementary performance—waitresses
and barmen;

(4) sequential performances—cooks and dishwashers;

(5) supervision—at several points;

(6) inspection—e.g. checkers and waitresses;

[(7) assistance—probably in kitchen, but not shown;]

(8) conveying objects and information—e.g. runners take food
from kitchen to pantry, and orders from pantry to kitchen;

(9) discussion—between supervisors;

(10) negotiation—between waitress and customer;

[(11) providing expert advice—no example here, possibly in
advice to customers.]

Each person working in a restaurant has to deal with one or more people, has to sustain certain social relationships and to exercise certain social skills. For example, the waitress has to deal in quite different ways with customers, barmen, cooks or runners, and a supervisor. The relationship with the cook in a small restaurant is difficult because the cook is of higher status and does not like to be given orders by waitresses. As already mentioned, Whyte found that this problem could

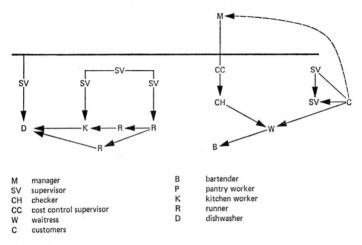

M	manager	B	bartender
SV	supervisor	P	pantry worker
CH	checker	K	kitchen worker
CC	cost control supervisor	R	runner
W	waitress	D	dishwasher
C	customers		

Fig. 8.1.

be solved by waitresses putting their orders on a spindle for cooks to deal with at their own speed; the same problem is eased in larger restaurants by the use of intermediaries. Quite different work-flow systems may be used in cafeterias or in restaurants, where the cook may do the cooking at the customer's table. Each work-flow system calls for specific social skills.

A manager may find difficulties in any of these socio-technical relationships and solutions may lie in any part of the system. Some difficulties may be solved by better social skills on the part of performers. Whyte, for example, found that some

191

waitresses found their jobs very stressful, and cried a great deal. One reason for this was that they were under constant pressure from customers, who wanted food that the cooks were not able to make rapidly available. Some waitresses, however, managed to deal with the situation by controlling, e.g. by persuading customers to have the food that was readily available. In other situations, the best solution may be to redesign technology, work-flow systems or the organisation, with social considerations in mind. This more radical social engineering may be a departure from traditional management practices. Nevertheless in many cases it is a prerequisite for the effective exercise of social skills by managers and the efficient running of the organisation.

Social organisation and technology

Woodward, Blauner and others have studied the kinds of social organisation found with different kinds of technology. Woodward studied the production systems and social organisation of one hundred English firms, and found at each of three levels of technological development a characteristic social structure which did not vary much with the size or organisation or the kind of work done.

Craft work and unit production. The craft worker either works by himself, or with a few helpers; working groups are small and cohesive with little need for supervision. There is a simple management hierarchy, with no specialisation between managers; it is a 'flat' hierarchy, with 25–30 men per manager; any specialists work in research and development departments.

Machine-tending and assembly-line work. Workers are in large groups, and social contacts on the job are limited. There is more use of incentives and machine pacing, and less close contact with supervisors. There are typically four levels in the hierarchy, and a more hierarchical structure, with 14–18 workers per manager. There is also more specialisation between managers, so that professional and technical people are involved in production.

More advanced technology. In oil refineries and similar plants there is a return to smaller working groups, less close supervision and better relations in the hierarchy, with 7–8 workers per manager.

Woodward found that the 'classical school' of management theory did not apply particularly well to any of these groups except for successful firms in the machine-tending and assembly-line unit category. These firms adhered to the 'classical' principles that each man should have only one boss and that he should know who he is. Orders should flow down from boss to subordinate and the information required to exercise control should pass up. Each man should possess a written job description and the organisation chart should show a 'chain of command' branching out from the source of authority and linking the individual roles. The span of control of executives should be 5–7 subordinates, that of first-line supervisors no more than 20.

With the exception of a larger span of control, Woodward found that five of the successful machine-tending and assembly-line firms followed these principles, whereas the six firms classified as below average did not.

Commercially successful small batch firms, or firms using process and continuous-flow production possessed a structure which differed from the classical model in many significant ways. In successful firms, responsibilities were not too clearly defined nor rigidly allocated. Indeed, rigid definition often appeared to be associated with failure. Similarly in the successful firms, functional specialisation, with its attendant needs to define line-staff relationships, was much less developed.

In process production spans of control were different too, the first-line supervisor having a much smaller span that in mass production but the chief executive having one much larger (an average of ten) than that recommended by the

N

classical model. In process production this picture of the span of control was also accompanied by an increase in the number of levels of hierarchy. 'Management by committee' was more and the chief executive appeared to function more as the chairman of a decision-making body than as an authoritarian decision maker.

Also the requirements of these different technical systems are attractive to some people and demanding for others. Different stresses are provoked by work in the different types of firm. Woodward found, for example, that in mass-production firms, where the technical variables were all known, increasingly precise controls were exercised. Production proceeded by drives and by setting even higher targets. Tight controls resulted in each manager down the hierarchy feeling pushed by his superior. Some managers accept and enjoy this sort of pressure.

Effects of innovation on social organisation

Burns and Stalker studied a firm producing rayon-filament yarn, an electrical company, and several electronics firms in Scotland and England. The management structure of the rayon-filament yarn factory is described by the authors as 'mechanistic'. Its salient feature was that tasks were highly specialised and each individual pursued them apparently separately from the rest of the concern, as though the work had been subcontracted. The technical methods, duties, and powers of each function were precisely defined. Most communications flowed upwards and downwards between boss and subordinate and very rarely laterally between colleagues. Instructions issued by superiors were contained in a book known as the 'Factory Bible'. Such a system allowed for little consultation but provided effective control, with each manager secure in the knowledge of what was expected of him, what decisions he could properly make and which matters he must refer to his superiors.

Because the firm had a stable routinised production process this structure was appropriate. The firm was commerically successful and the system, 'lubricated by a certain paternalism', worked smoothly and economically. There was no evidence that any individual felt aggrieved or belittled.

The electronics firms were expanding and also changing emphasis from the requirements of the armed services to those of civilian commercial customers. Whilst some of this change was into production of allied equipment (for example from radar into nucleonic instrumentation) other changes involved new products such as computers for data processing or business machines.

Burns and Stalker found that a structure to which they gave the name 'organic' was associated with success in these firms, whereas firms which clung (in some cases with 'strenuous effort') to a mechanistic system, were unsuccessful. Most of the Scottish firms studied 'failed to realise their expectations'. They were 'unable to adapt their management system to a form more appropriate to conditions of more rapid technical and commercial change'.

The 'organic' system is characterised by a freedom for individuals to work in their own way towards the common goal. Communications are lateral even between people of different rank. Functions and jobs are not clearly defined, and responsibility for decision-making is diffused throughout the hierarchy. In such a situation, constant and open communication become a pressing necessity. Meetings and committees for deciding policy and the exchanging and giving of information are essential, and people contribute their advice on the basis of their own specialist knowledge, irrespective of rank. The style of management is participative, consultative and democratic.

Burns and Stalker found various structures supporting the system. In one firm the 'Monday morning meeting' was a powerful instrument of the communication system. Heads of each of the major sections assembled with something of a ceremonial reaffirmation of solidarity and common purpose.

Skills with people

Organic structures again are attractive to many people but also create their own sorts of stress. Managers must learn to live with ambiguity and confusion, and risk becoming bewildered and insecure. This is a constant theme in Burn's account. As one foreman said, 'Of course, nobody knows what his job is here. When I was made foreman I was told "You'll start on Monday", so I came in and started. That was really all that was said.' The process of finding out proved unending. As a corollary, managers often had to get the job done through personal negotiation with other specialists on whom they were dependent. In these 'organic' systems, democratic leadership styles and skills in negotiating with colleagues were at a premium.

Miller and Rice, describing similar systems, mention the unfunctional steps which people in certain positions may take in the interests of group solidarity. They describe projects kept running unnecessarily or new projects initiated, not for their own sakes but to keep the group together.

This confusion and ambiguity may also lead to role conflict. In American studies it was discovered that 48 per cent of a sample of industrial employees experienced such a conflict for, example between the demands of management and the unions, between those above and those below, or between company and clients. In one study 35 per cent of managers were disturbed by lack of clarity about their roles. In another intensive study of fifty-three managers, all who experienced role ambiguity were tense and unhappy about their jobs. One source of role ambiguity is poor delegation of authority and responsibility by many firms' managers. Chapter 7 includes evidence indicating that job satisfaction is highest when subordinates participate in the making of decisions. Job satisfaction and productivity are influenced by the amount of discretion given to a junior, by the amount he is allowed to set his own sub-targets, make decisions and exercise control over resources.

Effect of organisation size and shape

Since the Industrial Revolution there has been a continuous increase in the size of working organisations, for technological reasons and to take advantage of other economies of scale. A number of comparisons have been made of work effectiveness and job satisfaction in organisations of different sizes. (By size is usually meant the number of people working at a particular location, though it may be necessary to take account of several plants together if there is centralised administration.) It has repeatedly been found that in smaller units job satisfaction is greater; while absenteeism, labour turnover, accidents and labour disputes are less, often by a large amount. However, no consistent relationship has been found with productivity; in some studies a curvilinear relationship has been found, with units of 1,500–2,000 doing best.

The shape of organisations can vary. They can be 'tall', with a small span of control and a lot of levels in the hierarchy, or they can be 'flat'. In a number of American studies comparing organisations in this respect it has been found that for organisations employing under 5,000 people, there was greater satisfaction in flatter organisations. In larger organisations there is some evidence that 'taller' hierarchies are both more productive and more satisfying.

The presence or absence of strong trade unions and the way these are integrated into the structure of the enterprise is another important factor in work efficiency and job satisfaction.

Effects of automation

The group of technical innovations known as automation have been affecting advanced countries so greatly since about 1950 that their impact has been called a 'second industrial revolution'. The distinctive elements of these technical innovations have been the use of cybernetic feedback and electronic computers. The rate of change is very rapid:

in 1960 for example, there were thirty-five process control computers at work in the USA, in 1966 there were six hundred.

There have been many studies of the effect of automation on the working group. In general, automation reduces the size of the labour force, creates new specialists, and calls for higher technical skill on the part of supervisors and managers. There is no overall upgrading of skill level, since many jobs are simplified. Many others, however, become more interesting and workers express increased job satisfaction.

The relation between supervisors and working groups is affected differently in different automated systems. In a power station workers became more autonomous. In a car factory automation increased the number of supervisors and led to closer supervision and more tension between supervisors. In the managerial hierarchy technologists become more important.

Although the introduction of computers may sometimes amount to mechanisation rather than automation, it is appropriate to consider here some of the studies on the effects of introducing computers. Mumford undertook a series of studies over a period of ten years, into the introduction of computers. She states: 'the computer technologist sees himself as replacing inferior manual data-processing systems with much better ones, geared to computer techniques. He does not appreciate that he is making what may be major changes in peoples' jobs, work satisfaction, career structure, security of employment . . . In other words he is unaware of the social by-products of his function.'

In two studies, one of a branch bank, at the time of installation of a new computer centre, and one of a medium-sized firm in the cattle-food industry, also introducing a computer, both managements encountered unexpected difficulties. The machines took longer to install than expected, which led to stress amongst the staff when pressed for faster results. The staff at both firms were dissatisfied with their pay, and in the cattle-food-producing firm there was evidence that health had started to deteriorate.

A majority of the clerks in both firms said the content of their jobs had changed. The bank clerks reported that the interest and variety of their work had decreased while the amount of work and standards of accuracy required, had gone up.

The introduction of a computer is only one specialised aspect of the effects of increasing mechanisation or changing technology. Woodward showed how a foreman's role changes when a firm moves from mass production to process production. In mass production he will be in charge of forty men. In process production he will supervise no more than ten men to whom he will be more of a technical resource than a boss, since the process itself determines the pace and the quality of the work. Chapter 7 included a description of the social changes which followed in the wake of technical change in a steel mill in South Wales.

A study made by the Tavistock Institute of Human Relations in the mines of north-west Durham compared the traditional way of mining with the organisation which followed the introduction of the Longwall cutter. Traditional single-place working was organised so that small self-selecting groups performed the three operations of cutting, filling and stone work. Although each member of the group had his special task, group members could substitute one for another. Pay was to the group as a whole. Relationships were harmonious and groups were self-regulating, needing no detailed supervision. This system of work produced considerable job satisfaction for the individuals concerned. Their work might be arduous and dangerous but it was skilled and challenging, and groups were highly cohesive.

The task changed radically with the introduction of the Longwall system of mechanised coal cutting. The new machine cut a long wall of coal in one operation and work was reorganised to meet the need to operate it economically. The old work teams were disbanded and the men divided into three shifts. Each shift performed one only of the three operations, and thus each man became a specialist at one part only. Each shift was paid separately and coordination had to come through management. The old system received a mortal blow, the job was deskilled, teams were split into new groups arbitrarily decided by the needs of the three separate shifts, and groups lost much of their former autonomy. As a result relationships between the men became poor, coordination of the three shifts proved very difficult to develop and productivity was far lower than had been anticipated from the use of more efficient machinery.

Effects of incentive systems

Different incentive system affect the social skills needed at work, especially those demanded of supervisors and managers. We shall briefly consider four different schemes.

Individual wage incentive. Here the supervisor is largely relieved of the need to motivate his men (though fear of rate-cutting, fear of running out of work, or simply desire to keep a steady level of wages may lead to restriction of output). On the other hand, the quality of work is liable to decline and inspection becomes more important. Also there may be friction between different workers, all of whom are seeking the 'best' jobs (i.e. those timed most generously) so that great efforts must be made to be fair. There is likely to be friction between management and men, or their union representatives, over the timing of jobs and the rates paid; this can be a source of frequent stoppages. Changes of working methods or jobs will be resisted, because men will have worked up a good speed and rate of earnings under the existing system and are unwilling to abandon it.

Group incentives. These are usually less effective than individual incentives, although with small groups on teamwork they may be more effective. Group incentives remove the friction between workers and foster the development of cohesive, cooperative groups. Thus these systems relieve the supervisor of two aspects of his job—motivating individuals and removing conflicts between them. However, he now has a more cohesive group to deal with, and negotiations over rates of pay and changes of work may be more difficult.

Measured day work. Under this scheme workers are paid a regular rate of pay in return for an agreed rate of work. The supervisor has to persuade workers that the rate offered is fair. If the work is machine-paced as on assembly lines, the rate of work is fixed, otherwise workers must be induced to keep up the agreed level of work. If a worker falls below this level the supervisor has to investigate and may have to transfer him to a lower grade or dismiss him. It is reported, however, that the measured day work system often leads to a better relationship in which workers feel more like trusted members of staff, with security and a stable wage.

The Scanlon plan. In this scheme there are departmental and company-wide committees which discuss methods of improving working methods and efficiency, and which decide the percentage of labour costs saved in this way which is to be paid as bonus (usually 75 per cent). Like other forms of 'industrial democracy' this seems to increase efficiency through generating more motivation and cooperation on the part of the workers. While in some ways it makes life easier for supervisors, it means that they now need skills of handling committees, and allowing workers to participate in decisions. Their power may be diminished to some extent as a result of the direct representation of workers on committees.

Planning a socio-technical system

Studies such as these show some of the ways in which task, technology, changing technical and market conditions, management structure and personnel policies affect human relationships in the organisation. These influences are inevitable;

different organisations successfully adjusting to different sets of circumstances are virtually certain to have differences in technology, management structure and so on, which in turn will offer the people they employ different satisfactions and stresses, and require them to use different interpersonal skills.

The studies show, however, that many of these effects were unrecognised in existing situations and not anticipated at times of change. Many posed unnecessary social strains. Some, indeed, such as the introduction of a mechanical Longwall cutter for miners in Durham, so damaged the social structure that the results offset the benefits of the new technology. Others simply exaggerate stresses which could be mitigated if fully understood.

Chadwick-Jones studied a tinning section of the steel industry, before and after moving location and changing from a manual technology to one using automatic controls. (The before situation is described in Chapter 7.) The men appreciated the better working conditions and less arduous work in the new plant, but the cost in individual and social satisfaction was very high. Manual technology had called for strongly knit, self-regulating and highly-supportive crews, within which an individual could progress steadily to higher skills. Men spoke of their old factory as home—as one worker said, 'Your heart is there.' The new technology was a continuous-flow process, requiring infrequent communication. The men's work consisted largely in watching dials and the sense of belonging to a team was lost. Chadwick-Jones comments that if the social dimension of organisations were studied before changes were made, it might be possible consciously to programme satisfying social patterns to accompany the introduction of technical and other changes.

Similarly Mumford concludes from her researches that the full benefits of computerisation are not being reaped, because the social results have not been anticipated and removed in the early planning stages. Unrewarding and boring jobs she says, should be designed out of the system. E. J. Miller and A. K.

Rice, after studying sales forces, an air line and a dry-cleaning business, propose a different solution. They advocate introducing opportunities for individual and social satisfaction where the nature of the work does not 'naturally' provide them.

There is of course plenty of evidence that where such opportunities are not provided, workers are likely to make opportunities for themselves. Where work study reduces the worker's task to that of an automaton, performing fractions of a total task or the residual work which has temporarily defied efforts at mechanisation, workers are liable to invent more amusing ways for passing the time. Anecdotes from a major automobile assembly plant describe practical jokes which operatives play to enliven their work. Glueing each others' tool boxes to the floor, or fixing cars so that stepping on the accelerator blows the horn and starts the wipers, provide human interest and variety in a day which intrinsically has none.

Similarly, Miller and Rice observed that the manageresses of the dry-cleaning receiving offices, 'identified with the customers, at the expense of the factory' where the cleaning took place. These manageresses were some distance from the factory and their social needs were not being met by any sense of belongingness to their own firm.

These reactions often amount to ingenious solutions to the individual's problems but are evidently unlikely to contribute to the objectives of the organisation. More conscious planning might more successfully relate the worker's needs to those of the whole. We now consider some of these planned solutions.

JOB ENRICHMENT

Job enrichment is an example of a deliberate attempt to 'humanise' work which had become devoid of interest. This has been done by job enlargement—each worker carrying out a wider variety of operations than before, as when assembly tasks are allocated to a smaller number of people. It has been done by job rotation—each worker learning to perform a number of different skills, and changing round periodically. It can be done by including elements of supervision in the job, making the worker partly responsible for planning, supplies, repair and maintenance, or making him something of an independent craftsman. Interest has even been added by varying the pace of work, for instance by the introduction of rest periods. In some jobs a sense of progress and of completing a meaningful task has been created by setting sub-goals and targets.

Other attempts at job enrichment have been concerned with enriching the worker's social environment. An early example of these developments was the expansion of the work of semi-skilled workers at IBM. Previously they had drilled one hole, afterwards their job included 'tool sharpening, the setting up of the machine for each new set of blueprints, a knowledge of calibration . . . the complete checking of the finished part'. In this and later studies it was found that job satisfaction was greater, production costs were reduced, and quality was improved, following the change.

Job enrichment also follows from the delegation of more authority down the line. Several studies made at ICI demonstrated that both job satisfaction and productivity increased when job holders were given more authority to manage their own work and were held accountable for results.

Decentralisation reduces communication problems, makes participation in decisions easier, and increases job satisfaction. In one study centralised and decentralised organisations were compared. A trend towards less absenteeism, turnover, etc., was found in the decentralised concern. Decentralisation is, of course, easier when sub-units are independent (e.g. shops), or can be given specific programmes of work to do.

COOPERATION WITH TRADE UNIONS

Humanising work involves recognising the conditions which human beings need if they are to perform a task both efficiently and with satisfaction. The situation requires the establishment of effective relationships between management and Trade Unions. Satisfactory industrial relations have always involved a mutual recognition of the value of the work of management and worker representatives, and the conditions needed to perform it.

Trade unions give power to workers and prevent managements misusing theirs. They provide managers with a line of communication which keeps them in touch with the social situation. Managements which recognise these advantages and accept the right of trade unions to exist and to recruit are moving from a situation of potential conflict towards one of collaboration.

Productivity bargaining, which attempts to relate higher pay to greater productivity, recognises some of the goals that management and workers share. The recognition is extended when the agreements involve worker participation in the planning stages. This may come to be seen as the critical factor. In one company recently a proposed bargain was rejected by the union after nine months' discussion, partly because they held that management had initiated most of the proposals without consultation. Thereafter three shop stewards and three managers spent four months' full time formulating together terms of the productivity bargain which eventually proved acceptable.

REDESIGN OF WORK-FLOW SYSTEMS

Extending beyond individual job enrichment, some imaginative experiments have been undertaken to redesign the work-flow system throughout an operating unit, taking into account the social implications of each job.

Following their study of the negative social effects produced by the Longwall cutter in Durham mines, described earlier in this chapter, the Tavistock Institute of Human Relations proposed a different work-flow system which retained the new mechanisation but recognised the merits of the old social system. This system, called the Composite Longwall Method, was adopted in certain pits. The men were regrouped, so that all three tasks were carried out on each shift, and each man needed to acquire and use all the skills of the different shifts. He had a responsibility to the total group, which was paid as a whole. This experiment proved highly successful, output rose in one pit, for example, to 5·3 tons per man-shift compared with 3·5 in the conventional Longwall organisation, and absenteeism fell dramatically.

Chapple and Sayles describe the reorganisation of the work-flow system in a sales department. Previously, orders were handled first by the sales department, and later by the credit department, which sometimes had to cancel orders at a late stage in the proceedings, after customers had been told that their goods were on the way. This system had led to consider-able conflict between the sales manager and the credit manager. Under the new arrangement, (1) the sequence in which orders went to the sales and credit departments was reversed; (2) all work connected with a single order was put under one super-visor, who was required to process it within the same day; and (3) both sales and credit representatives *took a hand in writing letters to customers when higher-level attention was needed.*

In the Ahmedabad textile mills in India, the introduction of automatic looms had not resulted in any increase in produc-tion. 224 looms were looked after by 29 men. The work was divided into twelve different tasks which related to one another in a very confusing way. A new way of organising the work created four working groups of equal size, three on weaving and one on maintenance. The groups were formed by mutual choice. Each group was collectively responsible for 64 looms, and performed its own ancillary services. The introduction of this new arrangement into one of the weaving sheds resulted in a 21 per cent increase in productivity and a drop of 29 per cent in damaged cloth; the new organisation was rapidly applied to other weaving sheds. The arrangement probably succeeded partly because workers belonged to small cohesive groups working on a cooperative task; and partly because the task was more varied and added up to a meaningful total performance.

REDESIGN OF ORGANISATIONS

A certain number of experiments have been undertaken to change the structure of a total organisation in order to improve social aspects of the work.

Sadler and Barry studied the technical and commercial aspects of work in printing firms where major changes in technical and commercial fields were taking place. They also analysed the organisational structure of the Jowert Press printing works. They proposed a new structure for the printing works which attempted to combine aspects of mechanistic and organic systems into a new whole, appropriate for the particular organisation. Their proposals combined close control by management (a salient feature of the mechanistic systems) with integrated communications across the organisation (an essential feature of 'organic' systems).

Each manager received a clear definition of his own function and its relationship to others. Simultaneously, however, work was decentralised, hierarchical control loosened and integration achieved through a series of interlocking management committees. For example, daily meetings were held which were attended by all production department heads; these meetings soon became known as 'wash houses'. Short-term results showed that managers were much clearer about their relationships and much more confident about their understanding of the work. The 1966–7 profit was 37 per cent higher than in 1963–4. Sadler and Barry considered this a 'remarkable achievement' when set against the trend of declining profits in the industry as a whole.

Guest supplies a case study in which a new plant manager succeeded in rehabilitating a low-producing automobile assembly plant by careful adjustment of its socio-technical system.

Plant Y comprised 200–500 workers. A central feature was a conveyor belt which wound for two and a half miles through the building. In 1953, when the research team visited it, Plant Y was failing to meet its schedules and costs were high. Pressure from higher management led to further dissatisfaction. The existing manager simply pressured his under-managers in turn. Perpetual crises meant no time to do any long-range planning. Meetings, if called, were solely to resolve crises, never for general information and consultation. Work-flow systems and organisation were inadequate and the technical system was obsolete in some areas. Worsening technical difficulties increased interpersonal conflicts and led to team and individual frustrations. These in turn led to further difficulties with inspection and line management. The actions taken by the manager worsened this situation throughout.

In 1953 a new plant manager was appointed—Matthew Cooley. Cooley began by reassuring people, individually and collectively, that he had heard people were not capable of doing the work but that he did not believe it and intended to disprove it. He introduced meetings for managers and service departments to consider long-range planning. Soon similar meetings developed spontaneously at lower levels in the plant. He encouraged supervisors to develop understudies and then saw that they were transferred or promoted. Line and staff began to see their problems as common and shared. He improved working conditions. Only after these changes did he introduce plans to reorganise technically so that operations, in their turn, became improved. By 1956, direct and indirect labour costs had gone down so much that Plant Y was the leading plant in the division. Its accident record, labour grievances, absenteeism and turnover had dropped dramatically.

Asked about the changes, the foreman laid as much stress on the reorganisation which had improved human relationships as they did on the elimination of technical bottlenecks.

They now felt free to suggest improvements and even described each other as being 'different personalities'. As one general foreman said, 'There were some people around here who I used to think were real bastards, but they have changed quite a bit.' Thus in one comment he indicated the intricate interdependence of technology, social patterns and individual social skills which Cooley had consciously recognised and had set out to modify.

Shell (UK) Ltd have recently pioneered a programme attempting to apply the concept of a socio-technical system to the practical management of a whole concern. As may be expected, the experiment has met with varying success, but the programme also produced some dramatic successes.

Check list for management of socio-technical systems

1. Could existing processes, work flow, technical systems or jobs be redesigned and made more satisfying to individuals and groups?
2. Are new technical or work-flow systems designed with social considerations in mind?
3. Does the existing organisation suit the critical activities, technology or commercial situation of the enterprise?
4. Are systems of pay appropriate and motivating?
5. Has size been kept to a minimum?
6. Have jobs been studied with a view to their enrichment?
7. Are trade unions playing a constructive role in the firm?
8. Has the organisation structure been re-examined within the past three years?
9. Does the structure of the enterprise aid the manager in the exercise of social skills?

Further reading

Readers interested in the general theory of socio-technical systems will find a useful and informative book in:

E. L. Trist, et al., *Organizational Choice* (Tavistock Publications, 1963)

Skills with people

Some practical uses of the general approach can be found in the following books:

Robert Henry Gest, *Organizational Change* (Tavistock Publications, 1962)

Paul Hill, *Towards a New Philosophy of Management* (Gower Press, 1971)

A. K. Rice, *Productivity and Social Organisation. The Ahmadabad Experiment* (Tavistock Publications, 1970)

Some effects of technology and technical or commercial changes on social structures are admirably described in:

Joan Woodward, *Industrial Organisation. Theory and Practice* (Oxford University Press, 1965)

Tom Burns and G. M. Stalker, *The Management of Innovation* (Tavistock Publications, 1966)

These books emphasise the need for social engineering:

Enid Mumford and Olive Banks, *The Computer and the Clerk*, The British Library of Business Studies (Routledge & Kegan Paul, 1967)

Enid Mumford, *Computers, Planning & Personnel Management* (Institute of Personnel Management, 1969)

J. K. Chadwick-Jones, *Automation and Behaviour* (Wiley Interscience, New York, 1969)

E. D. Chapple and C. R. Sayles, *The Measure of Management* (Macmillan, New York, 1967)

Philip Sadler and Bernard Barry, *Organizational Development* (Longman, 1970)

Books on job enrichment:

Lynda King Taylor, *Not for Bread Alone* (Business Books, 1972)

W. J. Paul and K. B. Robertson, *Job Enrichment and Employee Motivation* (Gower Press, 1970)

9

TRAINING IN SOCIAL SKILLS

As we have seen, the social skills of managers can have a considerable effect on productivity, absenteeism and other indices of organisational effectiveness. Until fairly recently long and carefully-devised training courses were given to manual workers, but virtually no training was given in this aspect of the work to the more highly-paid managers—they simply had to learn their social skills while growing up and while on the job. Over the last ten years, however, this situation has changed markedly, partly as a result of changes in society.

In the past, and to a very large extent today, people have learned social skills through their social experiences. They have learned to play roles appropriate to their age, sex, class and type of occupation. In a relatively static society, young people could be prepared for their future occupations with some assurance that these were the roles they would play. Sons of army officers and sons of directors of family businesses learned to take responsibility in a particular style which, if not always highly effective, was at least acceptable. The social upheaval after the war changed all this. The pattern of relationships in industry changed. People who had not been brought up to lead were given positions of responsibility. Many found themselves required to exercise social skills of which they had had no experience.

Meanwhile, research had shown that some ways of interacting with other people are quite ineffective in attaining the required objective, and that learning by experience is a very uncertain process. Many very experienced supervisors and managers were found to have learnt the wrong lessons from experience. For example, they had learned authoritarian styles of leadership which were ineffective with many post-war work groups.

211

Many interviewers fail to learn quite simple aspects of interviewing skills, such as how to deal with silent or over-talkative candidates. Years of experience had not taught them the verbal and non-verbal behaviours which help with these problems, and which can be taught in a few minutes. Yet these failures to interact effectively have considerable conse-quence. It is known now that the different behaviours of different supervisors, managers, interviewers, etc., produce variations in productivity of $2:1$ and of $4:1$ in absenteeism. In a study of sales girls Argyle and his colleagues found a ratio of $4:1$ between the amount sold by the fastest and slowest sales persons in the same departments. By showing the link between these results and the use of different social skills, such studies have indicated these specific social skills which should be employed.

Research has shown the value of both general and specific skills. These are the general skills; being the leader of a group, a member of a team, and dealing with individual subordinates, colleagues and superiors over a period of time, which have been described in chapters of this book. There are also a number of more specific skills for particular situations: being chairman and member of a committee, speaking at meetings, writing, and the different kinds of interview—selection appraisal and counselling. These skills are also described elsewhere in this book.

Recently there has been a proliferation of many kinds of training methods for managers, often including ingenious new methods for training in social skills. The demand for this type of training continues to grow. It must be acknowledged, however, that many of these ingenious methods have been launched with little evidence that they achieve their objectives. Sometimes indeed their objectives are not at all clearly defined. Similarly, organisations have adopted different methods without establishing conditions for determining their useful-ness. In the rest of this chapter we shall attempt a brief review of the main ways in which people are taught social skills, with any evidence that these teaching methods are useful. As a preliminary, however, we will review methods of assessing the effectiveness of this training and suggest procedures which should be followed by anyone attempting to make such an assessment.

Assessing the value of social-skills training

The method most often used by personnel managers is to ask those who have been on a particular course whether they found it useful. This method can yield helpful information for improvement of courses. Programmes can be adjusted in view of ratings accorded to their different components. However, it is far from providing information on course effectiveness in changing managers' behaviour. Most methods, if the instructors are reasonably skilled and sensitive, are accepted fairly enthusiastically, if only because course members are not prepared to admit to themselves that they have been wasting their time (and sometimes money). Note that it is not the usual practice of educationalists to ask children whether they find their maths or French lessons useful.

Another method of validation that has often been used is to compare the answers given to questionnaires completed by trainees before and after a course. This is not satisfactory either, since a course may simply change the way trainees talk or think about problems without affecting their behaviour. In one study it was found that the style of supervision of a large group of supervisors appeared to have been improved by a training course, though their behaviour had not changed at all.

A more satisfactory type of validation makes use of before-and-after measures of the behaviour of managers, or of measures of their effectiveness. Behaviour can be assessed by asking colleagues to make ratings on a number of rating scales. Ideally these should be 'blind' ratings, i.e. the raters should not know whether the person being rated is being trained or not, but this is difficult to achieve in practice. The reason for this recommendation is that the raters may believe the course to be effective or ineffective, and this may bias their judgement. Most of the studies of T-groups (T stands for training) described below used ratings of this kind. Alternatively, there can be before-and-after measures of some objective index of the manager's effectiveness. This is often difficult to obtain, and the indices of a number of different men may be difficult to compare.

In one such study 40 foremen were studied before and after a training course; there was an 8 per cent increase in output in their departments, none in those of a control group. In another study 87 supervisors went on a course to teach them how to introduce improved methods: during the following year they introduced an average of 1·85 improvements each, saving $1,240 per year each. Unfortunately, however, there was no control group in this study.

It is important that there should be a control group of similar managers who are not being trained but who are given before and after measures at the same time as the trained group. The expectation would be that the experimental group would be affected by the training experience in some way which would differentiate their 'after' scores from those of the control group. The way in which the before and after scores of control and experimental groups vary provides a valuable indication of the real usefulness of the experimental training. If the control group scores change to the same extent or in the same direction as those of the experimental group, the trainer must consider what extraneous influences (including test sophistication) may have operated on both groups to produce such results.

Besides obtaining some evidence of the immediate effect of training, the trainer is likely to need to know its long-term effects. Follow-up studies must be undertaken five to six months after the end of training in order to discount improvements which are only temporary. A large number of follow-up studies have been carried out, though many of them fail to meet all these requirements. An adequate procedure for assessing the value of a new training method is likely to involve:

(1) precise definition of the course members' training needs (in social-skills training this is likely to mean a precise definition of the way in which current behaviour needs to alter);

(2) precise definition of course objectives;

(3) selection of a control group of managers similar to the course members;

(4) development and administration of tests (questionnaires, observation, etc.) to administer before, immediately after training and some months after training completion, to both course members and the control group.

It is often exceedingly difficult to carry out all these stages satisfactorily in an industrial setting. The following example illustrates some of the problems.

A company became concerned at the high labour turnover of its (mostly immigrant) female shop-floor workers. This occurred particularly within the first month of joining. The company operated comprehensive welfare schemes and did much to help immigrants with housing, transport, etc. First-line supervisors were particularly friendly, motherly women who appeared very interested and helpful in their attitude to the operatives. However, after observation on the shop floor and discussion with superiors, personnel and training staff concluded that first-line supervisors were still not sufficiently in touch with their operatives. They had little time to speak to them away from the line and did not know how to give interviews which would encourage operatives to talk to them. In order to remedy this situation and, hopefully, bring down the labour-turnover figures, a much more detailed record of new operatives was introduced, giving information on family circumstances, home area, etc. These records were kept for three months and a programme of training in counselling interviewing was then introduced. All supervisors on two product lines received three hours' instruction, personal tuition and practice in counselling, and were then required to interview all new operatives at least once a week for the first four weeks after joining. They wrote reports on these interviews which were added to the detailed records already being kept. Two similar product lines were used as control groups. After six months the company had detailed records on all newcomers, three months without counselling and three months with two product lines being counselled by first-line supervisors.

Results were that labour turnover on all lines (experimental and control) dropped dramatically. This might be partly attributable to generally heightened interest in the problem, produced by the new records alone and by interest in the counselling exercise. However, the trainers had to recognise a major ulterior factor in the changed employment situation in the area. Also, about the time of the experiment the company introduced music-while-you-work and increased the number of immigrants promoted to first-line supervision. It was impossible to disentangle the influence of these various factors.

The outcome has been to retain and extend counselling training and requirements to all first-line supervisors, not because its value in reducing labour turnover is proven, but because it is appreciated by the supervisors, who find it makes the job more interesting and gives them better understanding of their operatives.

Whatever training courses are used or installed, a careful study should be made of their effectiveness, using the follow-up described above.

Methods of social skills training

In the process of growing up, people learn social skills by copying others and by direct instruction. Sex roles are learned, it may be surmised, primarily by copying, while table manners are learned primarily by instruction.

All the methods of social-skills training which have been developed can be seen as extensions of opportunities to copy others or to receive direct instruction. The social skills learned in adult work roles are still often taught simply by example. We have seen that this method is not always successful.

It *can* be successful, however, and indeed under the right conditions it can be a very effective form of training. It has one great advantage over all other forms of training in that there is no problem of transfer from the training situation to the work setting. Argyle has carried out a number of studies of learning social skill by experience. It was found that new sales girls, on average, increased their rate of sales over an eight-month period; there were enormous individual differences—some showed no improvement at all, and some became worse; the increase was greatest (58 per cent) in a department store using an individual incentive scheme.

There are several learning processes involved in learning by experience. There is trial and error; which is effective only if there is clear information on which behaviour is successful. Probably the main reason for the common failure to learn social skills by experience is that there is no clear feedback available. In another study 3,900 school children were asked to fill in twelve rating scales about 176 teachers to describe their ideal teacher and their actual teachers. The results were shown to half the teachers, who subsequently improved on ten of the twelve scales, as shown by later ratings compared with the control group. Feedback can work below the conscious level, as in operant verbal conditioning, or can act through the formation of verbalised cognitive controls which direct later behaviour.

Studies such as the one cited above show that training on the job can be successful if feedback is made available; observation of others is not enough to teach the skill. The trainee has to practise this skill himself and receive feedback on his performance.

Feedback can come in many forms. A sales girl may be

able to learn how to please customers and a speaker how to please audiences, from the responses the customers and audiences provide. The rating scales used in the study above provided valuable feedback. For certain skills in certain working conditions, videotape or audiotape recordings may be used. These tape-recordings provide valuable feedback (see below). People learning drama, public speaking, etc., frequently work with a coach or tutor who can comment immediately on any performance. In some clothing stores, buyers are trained to instruct the new sales staff, and school teachers in training both observe teaching classes and themselves give lessons under supervision. Certain conditions are required, however, if this type of observation and personal coaching is to be useful:

(1) the trainer must himself be competent in the skills he is teaching;

(2) he must have some understanding of these skills, so that he both provides a model and also is able to explain what he does and why;

(3) he must be able to establish a friendly, confident relationship with the trainee;

(4) he must have time to instruct; many working supervisors seem to be too busy getting on with the job to instruct trainees well.

In addition trainers probably need to be trained themselves. They can benefit from training in setting objectives for instruction, from some understanding of the learning process and the value of setting tasks within the trainee's capacity (see Chapter 3), and from training in observing and analysing the more subtle aspects of human behaviour (see Chapter 2).

Role-playing and simulations

This is one of the main forms of 'off the job' training in social skills. In simulated exercises, the trainee retains his own identity but acts in some artificial situation (e.g. a simulated interview or meeting) which resembles work situations in which he has to operate. In role-playing an additional feature is that the trainee may have to act the part of another person. Varying degrees of role-playing are possible; for example, the trainee may be required to 'be himself' but assume he has been appointed managing director; or he may be asked to take on the identity of another.

A number of follow-up studies have been carried out of the effects of role-playing on industrial supervisors and others. There is little doubt that the method is very effective in teaching specific social techniques, that feedback is important, and that videotape playback is very useful.

However, experience with role-playing and simulation has indicated several conditions necessary for it to be effective:

(1) The skills the trainee needs to acquire must be carefully defined and the role-playing and simulation exercises designed to relate to those skills.

(2) The exercises must resemble as much as possible situations which the trainee encounters in his working life. Although some trainees can benefit from apparently irrelevant exercises, most find it increasingly difficult to transfer any skills they have learned, the more remote the exercise becomes from their everyday experiences.

(3) Careful 'stage management' is required to ensure that the trainee sees the point of the exercise, knows what benefits he may gain from it and take his role seriously. This involves setting the exercise appropriately in the training course (see below) and good briefing and feedback.

(4) Accurate, detailed feedback on performance is essential. This can be provided by videotape and audiotape recordings. Some trainees improve their skills considerably simply by observing and hearing recordings of their own performance. In general, however, trainees need both accurate feedback and interpretation, discussion and guidance. This comes from the tutor.

219

(5) The tutor must himself have considerable social skill. He has to be able to comment on the trainee's performance in a way which increases the trainee's insight without destroying his confidence or making him defensive. One way of doing this is to use the unreality of the exercise itself to protect the trainee. ('Of course this was very artificial and not as you might have tackled it in real life, but did you notice that in this exchange such-and-such happened?', or 'Your impersonation of Big Brother was splendid. Let's see on the videotape the effect it had on your interviewee.')

In point (3) above we mentioned that role-playing and simulation exercises must be set appropriately in the training course. The trainer must take into account the level of skill, knowledge, seniority, degree of friendliness, etc., prevailing amongst his trainees. He needs to ensure that some familiarity and mutual respect is generated both between trainees and between the trainees and himself, before the exercises begin. Any exercise needs to be prefaced by specific instruction and followed by discussion.

So a vital first phase of role-playing is to provide a 'model' for the trainee to copy. This phase can take the form of a lecture, discussion, demonstration or film about a particular aspect of the skill. The establishment of a 'model' for the trainee to imitate is most important and is in itself part of the training provided by role-playing. Briefing for the exercise must indicate what skills are to be studied and must ensure that the trainees know the 'rules of the game'.

Trainees need time to study any background papers such as the application forms of a candidate for interview, or information about a personnel problem. Anyone introduced from outside to help in the exercise (e.g. an 'interviewee' in an interviewing exercise) also needs careful briefing as to how he is to behave and what point of view he is to put forward.

The feedback session, consisting of comments by the trainer, discussion with the other trainees and possibly playback of audiotapes or videotapes, should take place as soon as possible, preferably immediately after the exercise. The aim should be to draw attention, constructively and tactfully, to what the trainee was doing, to reinforce effective behaviours and to suggest alternative styles of behaviour where necessary. Recordings are helpful because they provide clear evidence for the accuracy of what is being said.

Course members can learn from observing these exercises, especially if drawn into the subsequent discussion. However, it is important that each course member should himself undertake an exercise.

A series of exercises is usually required to cover the range of skills employed in any one situation; also, each course member should perform at least twice (preferably three times) to overcome initial unease and consolidate learning. For this reason, useful role-playing and simulation takes time and the number of course members needs to be kept down. In courses on interviewing run by Management Training Aids Ltd., a range of exercises give training in questioning and in controlling the behaviour of the interviewee and in techniques of gathering information, counselling, negotiating, bargaining and persuading.

Role-playing can be conducted without the use of any specialised equipment, but it is greatly assisted if certain simple laboratory arrangements are available. An ideal set-up for interviewer training is shown in Fig. 9.1. The role-playing takes place on one side of a one-way screen, and is observed by the trainer and other trainees. A videotape is taken of the role-playing and a mirror may be used to film both people simultaneously. The trainer is able to communicate with the role-player through an ear-microphone.

Learning to chair a committee and to perform successfully in group discussion and problem-solving can take place more effectively and speedily through role-playing than through any other technique. A committee of trainees discusses some subject or is asked to reach a decision about some 'case

Skills with people

study' problem. Other course members observe the processes
of interaction, recording their observations systematically.
At the end of the discussion the trainer asks the chairman and
committee members to comment on their performance and
how they felt during the exercise. Observers and trainer, drawing

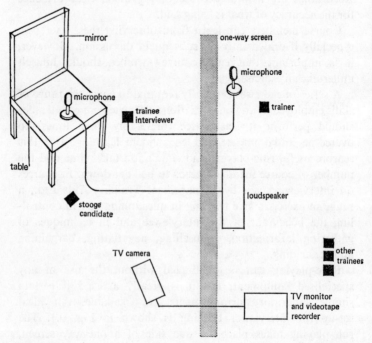

Fig. 9.1.

on their own recorded comments, then relate the committee's
remarks to what they themselves saw. A trainee learns from
observing and also from participating in a variety of exercises
in which he may act as chairman and play other roles.

The basic training technique described for training in
committee work can be adapted to help managers to become
more aware of group leadership functions. A leaderless group

may be asked to perform some practical task—such as to assemble two fifty-piece jigsaws in twenty minutes, or to build a tower from toy bricks. A form which asks questions about the task and socio-emotional communications displayed helps observers to analyse and so learn to control the task and emotional interactions in a group. Or a differently designed form can focus attention on to the leadership functions. A similar set-up can also serve for practising persuading skills, group members taking turns to present a case, either in the form of a prepared exercise or out of their own experience.

Sensitivity training

A different way of improving the individual's skills with people has been developed under the general heading of sensitivity training. Here the objective is not so much to study the effect of specific behaviours in achieving the individual's aims as to heighten awareness of the various ways in which people interact. In particular, of course, the individual is made aware of his own roles and how he tends to affect other people. The assumption is that recognition of these behaviours and their implications will help the individual to understand what is happening in various social situations and modify his own behaviour where necessary.

The goals of this type of training are thus (1) to increase sensitivity to interpersonal behaviour, (2) to show trainees how they are seen by others, and (3) to improve their general social skills in the work situation.

The basic form of sensitivity training is the T-group. This method of training has grown in popularity since its invention in 1947 at the National Training Laboratories in Bethnel, Maine. The essential procedure is for the trainer to meet about twelve trainees for a series of two-hour sessions. The trainees are told that their sole task is to study and discuss what is happening in the group itself, and that the trainer is there to help them to do this. There is a lot of direct comment on the behaviour of individual members: the trainer may intervene to provide such comments himself, or to explain what he thinks is happening to the group. In addition, there may be a number of ancillary exercises such as role-playing and lectures.

There have been a number of extensive and careful follow-up studies with control groups, and before-and-after analysis of behaviour on the job. Typical findings are that 30–40 per cent of trainees do improve to some extent in the three ways listed above, compared with 10–20 per cent of the control groups. However, the improvement may not have been due to the T-group training itself, since in all the courses followed up there were other kinds of training as well, such as role-playing. Furthermore, these follow-up studies used ratings by colleagues, which were not made blind, so that it is possible that the results were affected by their attitudes to the training.

The main problem, however, is that different trainees respond very differently to this form of training. In addition to the 30–40 per cent who benefit from it there are many who are apparently unaffected, and others who are upset by it and are found to be *less* effective after the training than before. It was found in one study that for every two that become more effective one became less so. In addition, there is a rather smaller group who are seriously disturbed by T-groups, and who need psychiatric treatment.

One solution to this problem is to do more careful screening of those going on T-groups or for trainers to be more watchful for signs of distress; however, part of the point of T-groups is to do something about authoritarian or other awkward characters in organisations—just the people who would be screened out. Another solution would be to reduce the level of emotional stress—some T-group practitioners do this, but others believe that the emotional arousal is necessary: 'It is a matter of what you are prepared to pay for psychically.'

There are now a number of variations and derivative training procedures developed from the T-group concept. There are different kinds of 'encounter groups' and training groups with very unusual exercises. The ability and training of trainers to run these exercises appears very variable, some being much better than others. It is our view that the benefits obtained from T-groups can be obtained less painfully in other ways. However, if there is an insatiable demand for this kind of experience, a rather conservative type of procedure should be followed, in which the following conditions are observed:

(1) screening of trainees likely to be upset;

(2) lowering of the emotional stress;

(3) learning of specific social skills, role-playing or other exercises;

(4) use of trainers who are socially skilled and therapeutic;

(5) use of more specific task material.

Traditional educational methods

Traditional educational methods—lectures, books and films—are widely used for the other kinds of training. They are cheaper and more generally accessible than the methods discussed so far; they may have special advantages for teaching the cognitive components of a social skill.

Lectures and discussion were the main teaching methods on early courses for supervisors and managers. Follow-up studies of some of these courses showed that the effects were either zero, or depended on senior managers practising the desired skills themselves. Manual skills certainly cannot be taught by lectures alone: learners must have a go themselves, at swimming, cycling or using a lathe. It appears that lectures and discussion can be very useful, if combined with more active methods of learning.

Lectures, particularly if related to discussion, can impart understanding of the relevant interpersonal processes and of the range of problem persons or situations likely to be encountered, and how to deal with them. Much practical, useful

225

information can be conveyed in a lecture on salesmanship or classroom teaching for example.

Reading is a very successful method of acquiring information and understanding; can it also convey social skills? Again, reading is valuable for conveying cognitive materials, which are needed for successful social performance. An important practical problem about the use of reading for social-skills training is the absence of appropriate reading materials. This book provides an introduction to a number of managerial social skills; Sidney and Brown provide rather more detailed materials on the selection and personnel interviews. A number of books of varying quality have been written on committees and meetings, most of which contain some reference to the interpersonal skills required.

Some programmed texts have been prepared which attempt to provide detailed training, e.g. in recognising and using different sorts of question. Stolurow's *Arab Culture Assimilation* is a tutor-text based on critical incidents which explain a number of features of Arab culture. It has been found that the ability of Americans to deal with Arabs can be improved by giving training with this text. In this instance some improvement in performance was produced by reading alone. However, the general rule seems to be that written materials should be closely coordinated with practical exercises, or should themselves include a description of the exercises. The learning is increased when reading is made part of the course in this way. Some written material is now available in the form of programmed texts to be used in conjunction with exercises. Examples are the texts on negotiating, prepared by Structural Communication Systems Ltd., and the self-administered questionnaires on motivation, based on McClelland's work (see Chapter 7) and prepared by McBer & Company.

Some of these materials require the trainee to view experience in the light of given intellectual concepts. Blake and Mouton, for example, analyse leadership styles in this way. The McBer series incorporates McClelland's findings on achievement motivation. It seems likely that many of the trainees who learn to recognise behaviours in different categories also heighten their general awareness of processes of social interaction and of their own effectiveness. Blake and Mouton and McClelland cite several training experiments where follow-up showed changes of behaviour in the desired direction.

Some use is already made of films in social-skills training. Sidney and Argyle provide five films on different aspects of the selection interview. Films on appraisal interviewing have been made by the British Institute of Management and the Civil Service Department, amongst others. There are no follow-up studies of the effectiveness of films for social-skills training, although they have been found to be successful for teaching motor skills—if combined with practice of the skill, and with discussion. It seems very probable that films could make a very useful contribution to social-skills training, and the full potentialities have not yet been used. They could act as a prelude to role-playing. They could be valuable in demonstrating conveniently the main personalities and problem situations encountered in a skill, and show the right and wrong ways of dealing with them. They could display some of the main processes of social interaction.

Some courses lasting three to six weeks give training in all these specific social skills and place them in the wider settings of the more general skills required by managers when running socio-technical systems. Lectures, case studies, discussion and project work then supplement the skills–training sessions. These courses are particularly valuable to intelligent 'high-flyers' and to younger men before moving from some specialist area (perhaps in research) to general management duties. The recently established business schools run longer courses still, which go further in the direction of teaching general management skills, but include very little training on the specific skills discussed in this book.

Skills with people

Special problems of training the socially inadequate

A considerable proportion of the members of any organisation are difficult in one way or another. Assuming a typical distribution of personality problems, some 8 per cent are likely to be neurotic and 1 per cent psychotic. A fair number, say 10 per cent, would score very low on measures of social competence, and perhaps the same number would be rather authoritarian. There will be some overlap between these categories and some of them will make a person less likely to rise to a position of much responsibility.

Ways of dealing with these difficult people include dismissal: this may in fact be the only solution to some problems (e.g. psychotics). In general, however, dismissal is resisted as a solution, both on humanitarian grounds and because those concerned may be very able in other respects. Another solution is to move these people to jobs where the social demands are less, or where they can do less damage; however, there are likely to be very few jobs which meet these requirements and carry any real responsibility in any organisation. A third solution is training specifically to overcome their difficulties. Here we consider the effectiveness of this solution in relation to some particular personality problems.

ATTITUDES TO AUTHORITY

Different organisations tolerate different degrees of respect for authority. It is, however, difficult to run any organisation in which a high proportion of people are entirely disrespectful of all forms of authority—as some universities have been discovering. It is, equally difficult to run a healthy organisation where a high proportion of people are excessively respectful of hierarchy and devote much energy to protecting their own status. Some British managers trained in the pre-war era found their leadership styles too authoritarian for success in the post-war world.

228

Some organisations have made great efforts, both in altering selection criteria and also in training, to deal with this problem. It is doubtful whether T-groups are very successful with authoritarians, though T-groups make them aware for the first time of what younger people think of them. Blake and Mouton have developed a kind of role-playing which gives trainees the experience of serving under authoritarians and other kinds of leaders. It must be admitted, however, that very authoritarian people are difficult to retrain, partly because they are convinced that everyone else is wrong and partly because they may have no respect for either trainers or psychologists.

SOCIAL ANXIETY

Some people experience acute social anxiety, either in specific social situations such as public speaking, taking the chair, seeing supervisors, or in virtually all social situations. This leads to their avoiding these situations and makes them ineffective at their job. One solution is psychotherapy, but this is extremely slow and expensive and is not effective with everyone. Recent studies show that behaviour therapy is more effective. The relevant form of treatment is 'desensitisation': the patient is helped to work out a 'gradient' of related situations, from the most to the least disturbing. He is then taught to relax his whole body and imagine the least disturbing situation. He then stops imagining, relaxes again, and imagines the next most disturbing, and so on. It was found in a study of the treatment of public-speaking anxiety that this method was more successful than psychotherapy.

INADEQUATE SOCIAL SKILLS

There is another group of people who simply fail to cope with social situations at work. They may be always quarrelling instead of cooperating, they may be unpopular, and be

229

generally avoided, they may be unable to deal with certain categories of people—superiors, subordinates, other social classes, females, etc., or they may be very ineffective on committees or other kinds of encounter at work. Such inabilities commonly stand in the way of a person being promoted, and may lead to his being dismissed; but they can be modified by appropriate training. Argyle has been treating neurotic patients and others with acute interpersonal difficulties for some years by means of role-playing and other exercises. What is done is to interview the trainee at length and to observe him in laboratory encounters, in order to build up a picture of what he is doing wrong. Then a series of exercises is devised to meet his particular needs. These include (1) role-playing of appropriate problem situations, with suitable stooges, (2) exercises in non-verbal communication and basic social interaction skills, (3) exercises in perception of others, and (4) tutorials on relevant aspects of social behaviour.

Design of an integrated training course

From the discussion above we can come to some conclusions about the best ways of giving social-skills training, at the three levels distinguished at the beginning of the chapter.

(1) Specific skills, such as selection and appraisal interviewing, running meetings, etc. The basic skills can be taught on a course of about three days, using a combination of role-playing, films, lectures and discussion.

(2) General social skills. These can be taught on the job by a trainer who sees the trainee in action. T-groups are intended to teach general social skills, and are successful with 30–40 per cent of trainees. However, the failure of T-groups with the other trainees makes us hesitant to recommend them. An alternative method of training in general social skills is a longer course of lectures, films, role-playing, etc., spread over a period of time, dealing with a wide range of social skills and interspersed with experience on the job.

(3) Training for cases of serious deficiency in social skill. We have recommended a variety of specialised training techniques, including role-reversal, desensitisation and tailor-made role-playing and related exercises.

Training in specific and general social skills requires carefully-designed training courses and it may be useful to indicate some of the principles of designing such courses:

(1) The basic unit of training, which can last for one long session or one day, should be a lecture plus discussion (if possible followed by film, tape-recording or demonstration), a period of role-playing and a session giving feedback on performance.

(2) The course should consist of a sequence of such units, beginning with the basic, elementary skills, and leading on to more difficult skills, including how to deal with the most common problems, persons or difficult situations.

(3) The trainers should be expert performers of the skills in question, and be knowledgeable about the non-verbal signals, and interpersonal processes involved. They should also be trained to comment constructively on course members' performance.

(4) Great care should be taken over designing the role-playing exercises to relate to the trainees' circumstances and the skills they need to learn.

(5) Great care is needed in briefing all concerned (including outside 'actors') on what is required in role-playing.

(6) Suitable films and written materials should be collected or prepared to supplement the lectures.

While basic principles and skills can be taught in quite a short time, proficiency at social skills also needs practice in the work situation. Good ways of providing this are by interspersing training with work, following up courses with projects and follow-up training on the job, as described earlier.

Check list for the manager

This list is intended for the manager who wishes to improve his own skills with people, or the skills of a subordinate. It is not intended for trainers or designers of training programmes.

1. What is the evidence that I am not (that X is not) achieving my (his) objectives in my (his) dealings with others?

2. What proportion of this failure can reasonably be attributed to my (his) lack of interpersonal skill (as opposed to, e.g. implications of company policies, organisational defects, trading problems, etc.)?

3. Can I define the area of failure in interpersonal skill (does it relate to particular situations, to particular groups of people, to people in particular roles, such as boss, subordinate, etc.)?

4. Can I define the nature of the failure (e.g. lack of information, lack of preparation, excessive desire to please, to dominate, etc., misunderstanding of role, inappropriate language or behaviour)?

The answers to these questions should help to ensure that the manager undertakes training with a clear idea of his needs and objectives. If a superior answers them on behalf of a subordinate, the subordinate must also accept the objectives before undertaking training.

5. Does the training proposed, whether a formal course or on-the-job experience, provide training in the skills required? Does it include a procedure or proposal for assessing the value of the training in terms of the trainees' subsequent behaviour? If not, can I devise such a procedure for myself (for X)?

6. Does the training proposed contain the elements of effective training—theoretical information, demonstration, relevant guided practical work, feedback on performance, adequate support material (literature, audio-visual aids)?

7. Can I check on the ability of the trainee to demonstrate the skills required and to provide constructive, acceptable advice on performance?

8. When considering a formal training course, can I check that the other trainees and the conditions proposed for practical work are likely to promote a realistic training situation for me (for X)?

Further reading

Evaluation and procedures for evaluating management training, including training in social skills, appear in:

Michael Argyle, Terry Smith and Michael Kirton, *Training Managers* (Acton Society Trust, 1962)

Peter Warr, M. Bird and M. Rackham, *Evaluation of Management Training* (Gower Press, 1970)

The advantages and limitations of T-group training are reviewed in:

L. P. Bradford, J. R. Gibb and K. D. Denne, *T-Group Theory and Laboratory Method* (Wiley, New York, 1964)

J. P. Campbell and M. D. Dunnette, 'Effectiveness of T-Group Experience in Managerial Training,' *Psychological Bulletin,* 73–104 (1968)

Methods of training the socially inadequate are discussed in:

G. L. Paul, *Insight v. Desensitization in Psychotherapy* (Stanford University Press, 1966)

An example of materials to train in a specific social skill is:

E. Sidney and M. Argyle, *Selection Interviewing Training Programme* (Mantra, 1969)

A method of training in the specific skills of leadership is described in:

Robert R. Blake and Jane S. Mouton, *Grid Organization* (Gulf Publishing, Houston, Texas, 1971)